Praise for *Risk*
the first book in the
God's Man Series

"I've always been an adrenaline junkie, so *Risk* instantly appealed to me. This book goes beyond the interesting and engaging descriptive stories to provide much needed prescriptive insight to enable men to live more boldly and powerfully. If you're up for being challenged in significant ways, read this book."

—MARK SANBORN, president of Sanborn and Associates Inc. and author of *The Fred Factor: How Passion in Your Work and Life Can Turn the Ordinary into the Extraordinary*

"Understanding the significance of the Christian message is of such great importance there cannot be too many ways to bring it to our attention. *Risk* is certain to inspire readers who long to give their all to a mighty cause, but who might miss the message if it were presented in a less passionate way."

—KEN BLANCHARD, co-author of *The One-Minute Manager* and *The Secret*

"Shocking are the Scripture's stories of men that took a risk! So are the modern-day accounts of men changing the world for God by taking risks. And then there's you… Are you risking it? This is a man's book for men— men of God ready to rip into the ends of the age. Dive into *Risk*!"

—DR. WAYNE CORDEIRO, senior pastor of New Hope Christian Fellowship Oahu and author of *Doing Church As a Team* and *Culture Shift*

"*Risk* is a book for men. It challenges us to faith, courage, and commitment. Kenny Luck tells the inspiring stories of men who risked everything to follow God. Don't miss this exciting and riveting challenge. It will stir your soul to action."

—DR. JERRY FALWELL, Liberty University in Lynchburg, Virginia

"*Risk* is a must-read for any man seeking significant change in his life. The book has great depth and momentum. Kenny Luck clearly communicates the message of what it means to completely sell out to God. Thank you, Kenny. I pray that all men everywhere will take the risk and trust God for everything."

—DAVEY BUHL, director of men's ministry at Christ Church at Grove Farm

dream

Have You Caught
God's Vision?

kenny luck

WATERBROOK
PRESS

DREAM
PUBLISHED BY WATERBROOK PRESS
12265 Oracle Boulevard, Suite 200
Colorado Springs, Colorado 80921
A division of Random House Inc.

All Scripture quotations, unless otherwise indicated, are taken from the Holy Bible, New International Version®. NIV®. Copyright © 1973, 1978, 1984 by International Bible Society. Used by permission of Zondervan Publishing House. All rights reserved. Scripture quotations marked (MSG) are taken from The Message by Eugene H. Peterson. Copyright © 1993, 1994, 1995, 1996, 2000, 2001, 2002. Used by permission of NavPress Publishing Group. All rights reserved. Scripture quotations marked (NLT) are taken from the Holy Bible, New Living Translation, copyright © 2004. Used by permission of Tyndale House Publishers Inc., Wheaton, Illinois 60189. All rights reserved.

Italics in Scripture quotations reflect the author's added emphasis.

Details in some anecdotes and stories have been changed to protect the identities of the persons involved.

ISBN 978-1-57856-987-8

Library of Congress Cataloging-in-Publication Data
Luck, Kenneth L., 1964–
    Dream : have you caught God's vision? / Kenny Luck.
        p. cm.
    ISBN 978-1-57856-987-8
    1. Christian men—Religious life. I. Title.
    BV4528.2.L83 2007
    248.8'42—dc22

                                        2007000462

Printed in the United States of America
2007—First Edition

10 9 8 7 6 5 4 3 2 1

SPECIAL SALES
Most WaterBrook books are available in special quantity discounts when purchased in bulk by corporations, organizations, and special interest groups. Custom imprinting or excerpting can also be done to fit special needs. For information, please e-mail SpecialMarkets@WaterBrookPress.com or call 1-800-603-7051.

*This book is dedicated in loving memory
to Lt. Commander William E. Luck and Delfina Carbulido Luck,
who have left our family to experience the dream
and are cheering their children on from heaven.*

contents

foreword

No man *likes* regret.

That's why we work so hard to make sense of our lives. We want to contribute, be meaningful. Sometimes we may sense our calling. But my problem, and the problem I see so often in guys, is that when we get serious about our legacies, the ways we go about finding them are shallow and performance oriented. And when we inevitably fail, we're left with the very thing we didn't want—regret.

I'm truly the worst at this. I grab what looks good in the moment, chuck the vision I really wanted, and realize only later what I've done. Recently, I began to wonder if this pattern is a reflection of me and my own desire for significance, or if it's a broader problem. After all, our instant-gratification, media culture convinces many of us to trade our dreams for the flashy and extreme. But when I consider how I've tried to escape regret and selfishness, and when I aim for true significance in my life, I realize I'm searching for a vision that's uniquely mine. And to do that, I need the right focus coupled with the right disciplines to sustain my motivation and move me in the right direction.

Oh. And did I mention the journey can't be boring?

I'm a hare who needs to think like a tortoise. The bunny will torch out and lose. The tortoise will finish the race. But that old turtle just doesn't grab my attention. He isn't fun to watch. Now, he does have a plan, and he's going to work it. And I admire him—I'd love to have that sure, steady character—but that isn't the kind of dream for me. I'd need multiple races to keep going that long because, like the hare, I'm always looking for the next goal, and the next, and the one after that.

But what if there's a way to fuse the turtle's character with the rabbit's passion? Who do you think would win that race? I want the passionate pursuit of the greatest vision for my life to be one that's loaded with excitement—but also built on a solid foundation. And as a hare, I need a plan that prevents me from skipping out one lap before the finish line.

We all experience obstacles in our dream of significance, to be and do something great. It's a nearly universal struggle to first find the dream, to stay with it, and to express that passion in the right ways. So here it is, in this book, the personal plan I've developed for truly significant living.

But let me confess at the outset: I was embarrassed to find the answer. I had missed it before—and it was there all along! You know when you're desperately looking for your keys, and then you look down and see them in your hand? This solution was that sort of shocking simplicity for me, the kind that reveals God's design so perfectly.

If you start applying this plan, I believe you'll make some shocking discoveries of your own. Feel free to e-mail me your thoughts. I'd love to hear from you.

Dreaming big with you,

KENNY LUCK
Founder, Every Man Ministries
Men's Pastor, Saddleback Church
kennyl@everymanministries.com

chapter 1

when God gives glasses

It is imperative that we know what it means to see, to hear, and to discern the things of the world to which we truly belong.

—MARK CHIRONNA

They are all staring at me.

Lori's wig is crooked. She's got a nine-year-old and is losing her battle with cervical cancer. To her left is Paul. He has pancreatic cancer and his wife, Evelyn, will lose her partner of forty-seven years in only four weeks. To his left is Beth. She just had a lumpectomy, lost her left breast, and is beginning a chemo regimen. Her engagement to sing her first solo concert at the Kennedy Center has been canceled. The other side of the room is not looking much better. Bill's abdomen is distended and he looks as physically uncomfortable as his wife does. They don't even have the comfort of a diagnosis. To their left are Maya and William. They just got run over with positive biopsy results and resemble emotional road kill: blank eyes staring at speckled tile and no signs of life. Sitting next to them is Mike. The wrapping on Mike's head can't mask the huge divot of missing skull from a surgery that removed a glioblastoma from his brain.

> *As I look at him, I can't fend off the thought that he's a goner.*

As I look at him, I can't fend off the thought that he's a goner. His kind of cancer is not the kind you survive. His chin is in his chest and I can't see his face. His new wheelchair makes him slump. I can't tell whether he is doing well today or not.

By contrast, Michelle is supremely visible. Outwardly perfect, she is flanked by her two perfect girlfriends. Their perfect world, perfect nails, and perfect makeup suggest all is very well. But Michelle's insides betray her outsides. Blond and beautiful outside, but bellicose and bitter on the inside. She is losing her fight with an aggressive breast cancer. The trip to Japan to explore experimental therapies was a failure and she's back with us in Orange County. On this night, in this room, the big C is defeating the OC.

Oh, and did I mention? They are all staring at me.

The year was 1993, and I was twenty-nine years young. I was attending seminary, working full time, and had been assigned a clinical pastoral rotation on an oncology unit. One evening a week we met in the basement of the Western Medical Center in Anaheim with about thirty cancer patients and their families or friends. To describe this time as a defining moment seems to cheapen this chapter of my life, but it captures the ethos of the year in which my world was beautifully ruined by God. It was a year of first-time encounters with reality:

- first time I was afraid to show up for work
- first job in which mortality was a daily reality
- first sustained connection to cancer and its victims
- first encounters with true despair and imminent death
- first exposure to "unfixable" emotions
- first big crisis of faith
- first funeral
- first time I caught a clear vision of life and heaven

What did I *see* for the first time?

- I control nothing.
- Trauma dissolves the trivial.
- Relationships define riches.
- Personal discomfort leads to discovery.
- Reality, however painful, is where we find eternity.
- God's vision for me is different from my vision.
- Physical poverty produces spiritual clarity.

A cancer support group was God's agent of new meaning and purpose in my life. I didn't like His choice, but He didn't care. He let me borrow His glasses. He decided that's the kind of reality I needed to get clear in order to see Him and, in the process, see myself. I saw that Kenny likes sanitized, sanctified, and tidy. He prefers comfortable and predictable, like any good adult child of an alcoholic. I saw a man who freaks out and wants to run when the environment gets emotionally negative or out of his control. God showed me how I prefer the focus to be on someone else who needs help. I don't like feeling helpless. He pointed out my affection for regular outward results, numbers, and success you can quantify.

He made me face my tendency to rewrite reality to make people feel better. He pointed out how I wanted to teach more than be taught—to be someone's solution versus process an issue. I like prescriptions that cure and solve, not processes that end poorly or, God forbid, remain unresolved.

He showed me that it's possible to prefer heaven so much that it leaves little room for the real emotions and problems of earth. He showed me just how much I like my version of serving God and being God's man. But my version wasn't working for Him. It was time for an Etch-A-Sketch moment, or better, an Etch-A-Ken moment. I turned my screen upside down and erased the picture that was there. I didn't want to start fresh, but it happened.

Glad it was me and not you? Not so fast. You're going to get to wrestle too. God wants to erase what you've drawn on your Etch-A-Sketch and instead draw His dream for you.

Will you let Him?

The Big Oak Tree

In my neck of the woods, Live Oak Canyon Road is famous. It's famous for its curvy sloping turns. It's famous for the large and beautiful heritage oak trees that canopy its spirited descent past Cook's Corner. It's famous for its horse ranches and a steakhouse. On weekends, it's home to scores of Harley-Davidson riders and car enthusiasts alike. This road has it all. It calls out to you to roll down the windows, blast your music, and step on the accelerator. Travelers never forget this little stretch of heaven, and campers know it as the entry of passage to O'Neil Regional Park.

But you might start to notice other things along Live Oak Canyon Road, things that tell another side of its personality. Little crosses and bouquets of flowers enshrine some of the larger trees. Abnormal gouges mar the woody flesh of others. On certain days, you might see people standing side by side, staring at or praying next to one of the big oaks. And on others, you might see a police car on the road, an officer instructing you to turn around. There's been another fatality.

> *Live Oak Canyon Road is famous for a lot of things, and one of them is death.*

Live Oak Canyon Road is famous for a lot of things, and one of them is death.

The brutal fact that belies the beauty of this road is the invincibility of oak trees. Oak is hard and oak trees bend for no man.

My neighbor Gary lets me borrow his spare Harley Road King, and we ride down Live Oak Canyon Road. I feel free, empowered by the throttle, more confident with each shift of the gear box. I gain speed, control, and comfort as I climb to cruising speed. Yet there is a sense that danger is just one slip away, and my acuity for my surroundings is heightened. I am especially aware of the oak trees. It's a weird combination, but a necessary one if I am going to enjoy this ride. I have to respect the oak trees. I have to be sure of that. I wonder if everyone who has perished on this road was feeling the same way before something went horribly wrong. Elation, then devastation. You have to be alert and respectful while enjoying the beauty.

Live Oak Canyon Road is the dream of being God's man. It's so inviting, so attractive. It's beautiful and challenging. It's also very dangerous when you take too many liberties, look too long, or begin to think you have it figured out. It's not hard to get loose in the corners. It's easy to outpace the road. New tires can breed overconfidence. It's tempting to push for more speed when caution is in order.

It's easy to feel like you have this course wired.

And just when it feels familiar—you guessed it—a million little pieces.

God's vision for you is solid, invincible, and has been in place for a long time. It is an oak tree. It is unstoppable. Only arrogance or ignorance would attempt to displace it, try to cheat it or ignore it. And yet we do. We presume to design what we will become in Him. We chase our fantasies over His chosen vision. We forecast and fashion our lives in our own image. We reengineer ourselves for cultural acceptability. We shape our dreams around our own insecurities and dysfunctional tendencies.

And then there is the fatal error: we take God's plan for our lives and make it something to be conquered. We get behind the wheel and take over. I wonder what God thinks of all our presumptions, our engineering of His plan for our lives.

> *God's dream for us is not something we chase; it's something we become.*

The dream we have for ourselves is unnatural. It is not God's dream for us. God tells us in numerous places and in numerous ways, "My version of your future is not your version. Your dreams are not My dreams. Your paths are not My paths. Your ways are not My ways." If salvation is not a result of what we do, then why would we think His vision of greatness as a man would be dependent on our exploits?

God's dream for us is not something we chase; it's something we become.

God set Samuel straight when he set about looking for a God's man among Jesse's sons: "Do not consider his appearance or his height, for I have rejected him. The LORD does not look at the things man looks at. Man looks at the outward appearance, but the LORD looks at the heart" (1 Samuel 16:7). God's dream for your life is not external, designed to impress. It's not internal, a value or a purpose. It's not even a spiritual discipline or set of beliefs. God's dream for you is a heaven-owned vision of greatness, a God's man image built upon that of the God-Man.

You have known this and felt it inside of you ever since you were a little boy. It's time for all of us to recapture it.

The Dormant Volcano

I see the volcano in my eleven-year-old son, Ryan.

He's dormant one minute and exploding with magma the next. It seems so random. All of a sudden he blurts, "Wouldn't it be great if our car could fly like both a plane *and* a helicopter?" His creative outbursts don't apologize for defying modern physics. They unshackle him from the realities of the earth that are boring, cumbersome, or rule bound. He's thinking, *Just give me some technology and an Xbox controller and I'll take us home Ryan-style.*

I love these creative moments and visions. Not because they're impractical but because, in a more masculine sense, they satisfy. They thrill. They problem solve. They defy simple logic. They unshackle. They satisfy. And all these visions inside that young brain are like ours—before they got buried. The common denominator of Ryan's visions is that if they were reality, they would result in a deep gasping for air. An unforgettable sensory experience. Soiled shorts.

When life isn't going well, we long for a better life. Heck, even when life seems to be perfect, we long for more. Admit it! We feel this pull to rearrange reality, to experience freedom, to gratify deep longings inside. Take it from Ryan. That's why he blurts these things. They are bursting dreams: unorganized thoughts, sensations, and images that need to break free. They come from down in the core, cooking and bubbling below the surface, the mysterious magma pushing upward to reshape our reality.

Look at yourself and the men around you and think, *Kilahuea.* Kilahuea (kill-uh-WAY-uh) is the most active lava-producing volcano in the world. It used to be dormant. In Hawaii, it started exploding in 1953 and again in 1983. It hasn't stopped flowing lava since, according to the U.S. Geological Survey. All men are Kilahuea, bursting with bright orange visions and dreams that will challenge reality and shake up the landscape forever. Some men have magma close to the surface. Some have theirs buried deep. But make no mistake—it's there, it's alive, and it's put there by God. That magma is called eternity. It's called His image.

> **dream fact**
> *You were made to dream creative visions, because you were hardwired for more.*

You were made to dream creative visions, because you were hardwired for more.

You don't have to accept less or feel bad about wanting to transcend reality. You're Daddy's boy—you are made to be great like Him.

Between Reality and Glory

Yet there's more to this natural creative vision than just challenging reality. The real driver is to become an agent of greatness. The means are second-ary. Talk to Ryan—the car-plane-helicopter is just the vehicle. *He* is the pilot who will crawl out of the cockpit of this revolutionary aircraft, pull off his helmet, and wave to the crowd. When little boys play, it's all about the glory. Regress for a minute to when you were ten. I had a scrapbook filled with cut-out pictures from old *Sports Illustrated* magazines. Images of men in the midst of glory, poorly cut-out tailbacks breaking free from tacklers, receivers escaping gravity to catch a pass, two sets of opposing lineman about to go to war on fourth and goal. Where are all these men headed? Glory. Flip to the next page. Same thing. It's a boy's personal dream museum: larger-than-life men doing something great which lands them in places where glory resides. In my mind, that was me in those pictures someday!

So what happened to the pictures? Well, they were changed.

Or maybe they were replaced.

I don't know exactly when it happened, but time was not a friend to my early visions of greatness. I had to grow up. We all did. As this happened, our visions of glory were tempered and morphed to reflect the realities of life. Time wasn't always on our side. The events of life got in the way—divorce, death, disappointment, unreasonable standards. We started to lose hope. Our loneliness split our loyalty and disintegrated our faith in real relationships.

The pure, ideal visions simply went away and were replaced with insecurities and fears which led not to dreams but to fantasies that soothed our hurts. Escape and relief relegated greatness to just getting by. Glory was simply not reality anymore.

Reality won. Glory was lost.

This war between reality and glory happens in cycles throughout our lives. The magma of our dreams pushes its way up again. There are a few sparks. Going off to college. Graduation. Career. Promotions. All visions of heading off for glory. Then reality nudges in, reshapes things and blocks

dream fact
It's out there. In Africa maybe. Or is it?

our path to real glory. Our vision gets tackled for a loss. It's fourth and long, and we have to surrender the ball. The energy drains out. Gravity wins. Earth pulls us down. We may have heard the rumblings, but we never saw the bright orange magma, the awesome power we had planned to see. It fizzles. Just say the word *fizzled*. Catch my drift? I don't like it when my dreams fizzle. Which dreams?

- being great
- doing great things
- winning battles

- changing lives
- contributing
- maintaining integrity
- giving generously
- influencing men
- being good
- performing under pressure
- succeeding
- great relationships
- a legacy for God
- slaying giants
- rising above circumstances
- conquering fears

There you have it. Those dreams are the substance of my magma. When I am not the man I should be, I long to be this man, the man I ought to be. When I don't do the things I should, I long to act differently so I can win at life. I want to do all that great stuff, but how can I with all my limitations? I would have to live somewhere else. Possess a different station in life to accomplish that kind of stuff! Become someone else.

Reality says that 5 percent of life is extremely satisfying. Another 5 percent is extremely disappointing. The rest—the other 90 percent is just life, plain peanut butter and jelly. The dream for me and the glory that goes with it reside somewhere else, in some other life, some other place, far away from the peanut-butter-and-jelly life. It's somewhere out there for the select few and uberspiritual.

In Africa maybe.

Then a little voice whispers, *Or is it?*

It's at this point I need Ryan. I need to recall what it means to dream and
have a simple vision that can transform, thrill, and satisfy. I need to blurt,
"Wouldn't it be great if my regular reality were the pathway to glory?
What if this life could cause my dreams of being great to come true?
What if this ordinary life could achieve glory every time? Yeah, every
time! That's why it's called a dream. And we can realize it if we have
the courage to face it and allow God to transform the ordinary.

Ready to dream again, Kilahuea?

> I keep asking that the God of our Lord Jesus Christ, the glorious
> Father, may give you the Spirit of wisdom and revelation, so that you
> may know him better. I pray also that the eyes of your heart may be
> enlightened in order that you may know the hope to which he has
> called you, the riches of his glorious inheritance in the saints, and his
> incomparably great power for us who believe. (Ephesians 1:17–19)

God's dream for you is not a matter of availability or proximity; it is a
matter of connection and awareness. It's already there for the taking! If
the apostle Paul were an island boy like me, it might read, "I am asking
God to tsunami you with His dream for your life and explode His power
within you."

The dream to be great and to do something great is put there by God.
Don't be ashamed of it; embrace it in Christ! It's time for a fresh vision of
who He has called you to be. It's time to seek the glory which is yours for
the taking right where you are. Embrace these five DREAM principles
for every God's man:

- **D**ecide to let God decide for you.
- **R**eside in the glory of your reality.
- **E**xchange your vision for God's.
- **A**ccept God's process.
- **M**ove your borders in continual growth.

Decide to Let God Decide for You

God's man lets God decide the dream. When I was working in that cancer unit, God's dream for me looked like this recipe:

- 1 cup of hospital assignment
- a handful of mixed cancers
- 3 tablespoons of unfixable realities
- 1 large crisis of faith (unpeeled)
- 1 ton negative emotions and loss
- Mix in doubt and stir thoroughly.
- Bake at 350 degrees for one year.
- Remove and serve with humble pie.

The minute I start letting feelings, culture, or others decide what defines my dream, I am cooked as God's man. Jesus is our Master Baker on this one. "My Father, if it is possible, may this *cup* be taken from me. Yet not as I will, but as you will" (Matthew 26:39). Jesus let His Father decide what the dream for His life on earth would be. The dream didn't depend on His circumstances, His rights, His parents, His friends, His critics, or His feelings. It's no surprise then that the exact dream God has for you is in the mold of His Son. "For those God foreknew he also predestined to be conformed to the likeness of his Son, that he might be the firstborn among many brothers" (Romans 8:29). For every God's man ever born, this has been the plan, and this is the process we are all engaged in: becoming like our firstborn Brother, Jesus. We'll define the specific targets later, but for now, resolve to let God decide what goes in His recipe dream for you.

Reside in the Glory of Your Reality

Your reality is God's glory. Everything that is happening in your life—especially the stuff you want to keep a secret—is an ingredient in God's greatness. You might be thinking, *I don't want God to use that!* God's reply is, *That is exactly what I want to use.* God is eager to use your now-life, not your cleaned-up version. To fuel the dream, He prefers struggles over strengths. One gives Him glory, the other gives you glory. Yep, it's the spots on the lepers and their utter helplessness that got God excited and put the clean to shame. Got some ugly spots dotting the epidermis of your life right now? Got old spots and scars that the masks can't cover? God is operating in your uncomfortable realities today, not in the ideal future. Sound weird? You're in good company.

> As he went along, he saw a man blind from birth. His disciples asked him, "Rabbi, who sinned, this man or his parents, that he was born blind?"
>
> "Neither this man nor his parents sinned," said Jesus, "but this happened so that the work of God might be displayed in his life." (John 9:1–3)

Reality is where glory resides. I know this from personal experience. If the disciples saw me as a seventeen-year-old, they would have asked, "Lord, who sinned, this man or his parents, that he should be doing drugs, looking at porn, lying, and making choices that will ruin his future?" Jesus would reply, "This is happening so that the work of God can be displayed in his life." And it has. Feeling better?

Alcoholic dad. Codependent mother. Repeated dysfunctional choices. Good and bad desires in conflict. Destructive habits. Dishonesty in my marriage. This was my unsanitized reality. But God did not remove it when He came into my life; instead He used it to deliver the dream. My awful realities, tendencies, and testimonies became His glory, His dream as Christ replaced the crud inside of me. The chump becomes a champ. Take out Kenny and replace him with Christ.

> *Take out Kenny and replace him with Christ.*

The result? God's man bears His reality, and others see the transformation and begin to believe!

> He lifted me out of the slimy pit, out of the mud and mire; he set
> my feet on a rock and gave me a firm place to stand. He put a new
> song in my mouth, a hymn of praise to our God. Many will see and
> fear and put their trust in the LORD. (Psalm 40:2–3)

Reality is where glory resides.

From what can't you seem to deliver yourself? Don't run from reality; let God bring glory through it.

Exchange Your Vision for God's

Some men envisioned their lives would turn out a certain way, but those plans fell apart. Some of these guys feel ripped-off and angry because they were supposed to achieve their dads' visions. They felt controlled and forfeited their chances to choose. A lot of men were wounded so badly by their dads, they chased the opposite vision in response. Resenting or trying to please those wounding fathers only led to anger, and they ended up becoming just like them. Others were trained by tradition. Mom and Dad taught them that their lives should look and feel a certain way, and that's exactly what they turned out to be. Tradition triumphs over the individual. But that's not the man's life, it's his parents'. Still other men have built their lives to directly reflect their insecurities and masculine fears. These guys attach to cultural definitions of success, stockpiling pleasure, power, or possessions to gain what they could not find in their early relationships. This kind of life almost always fragments relationships and leaves men starving for intimacy and connection. In each of these cases, the dream leads to emotional, relational, and spiritual bondage. They are the false dreams that involve chasing, wishing, and hoping. They are not Christlikeness. They are empty and void of spiritual power because they are the man-made fantasies, not the God-made dream.

If you're God's man, the contract reads like this: "So from now on we regard no one from a worldly point of view. Though we once regarded Christ in this way, we do so no longer. Therefore, if anyone is in Christ, he is a new creation; the old has gone, the new has come!" (2 Corinthians 5:16–17). This means:

- The man-made versions of greatness are supposed to be thrown out.
- The "in Christ" vision mutually excludes the world's self-serving visions.
- Self-preservation and security must cease being a vision—you cannot be your own cause if you are God's man.

- It's not just a wave of new behavior but new waves of thinking and believing that never cease. God doesn't stop creating the new you. It's continual and dynamic.
- Christlikeness becomes all.

Exchange all other visions for God's—the one in Christ.

Accept God's Process

God is not very product oriented. That's a bummer for most men, including me. We like to look at what we've done. Leader-coach Walt Henrichsen puts it this way:

> God is not as interested in how holy you are as in the degree to which you are engaged in the process of application. If you are new in Christ with a great deal of carnal self still present in your life, but you eagerly seek to do His will, you are pleasing to God. If you have known Christ for years, but have ceased seeking to grow in Christ through the process of application, you are not pleasing God.[1]

Surrendering to the process is not a masculine gift. In fact, the Bible is littered with stories of leaders who ran ahead of God because they were impatient. And they paid the price. Both ancient and modern men of faith can relate to the proverb, "There is a way that seems right to a man, but in the end it leads to death" (Proverbs 14:12). When the timing and means are not as we would have it, or the results feel unjust or unacceptable, we tend to fight the process. Fighting an unjust process is not a bad thing. Fighting God's process of making you the man He created you to be is disastrous. Avoiding that sinkhole takes guts and a belief that God is more capable of deciding what's needed and best for you at any given moment.

God's dream of molding you into the image of Christ will involve discomfort, conflict, loss, and pain. Stick with me.

For so many years I trained myself to preempt, deflect, or deny entry of these growth opportunities into my life, and I missed God's process all together. Eventually, because He loved me, He cornered me through circumstances until the pain exceeded my fear. He pinned me. So many times, I wish I had done the hard thing and engaged the conflict or the process earlier. I should have trusted God to work instead of bailing and avoiding. I wish I had willingly volunteered rather than waited to comply. You might be there right now. If you'll surrender and do the exact thing you don't feel like doing, you'll be glad you did.

> **dream fact**
> *God's dream will involve discomfort, conflict, loss, and pain.*

We will unpack this more later. For now, just remember this: nothing happens to you unless it passes from God to you. And if it comes that way, it comes with a purpose—to make you like Christ.

Move Your Borders in Continual Growth

The ambition of God's man to become like Christ requires aggressively pursuing that one ambition. We need to constantly stretch the borders of our growth for the duration of our life on earth. Jesus didn't mince words or parse verbs on the whole topic of growth. He said either you are growing or you are dying—fruit or no fruit. There is no middle ground. That's why many men who e-mail me are so incredibly down: they've chosen to coast in their spiritual lives, and then they've found they are not coasting, but dying! They stopped abiding in the vine of Christ, disconnected from His process, and have no source of nourishment for their convictions. God's dream for God's man always involves personal growth and fruit. He is increasing; I am decreasing.

More Christ, less Kenny. More humility, less pride. Less self, more service for others. And so on…

God's man prays the brave prayers of continual growth. Prayers like Job's emerge when he opens his life up to God's inspection and gives his Maker freedom to rewire his life. He keeps moving the borders, giving God more and more freedom to change him.

> If I have walked in falsehood or my foot has hurried after deceit—let God weigh me in honest scales and he will know that I am blameless—if my steps have turned from the path, if my heart has been led by my eyes, or if my hands have been defiled, then may others eat what I have sown, and may my crops be uprooted.… Then may my wife grind another man's grain, and may other men sleep with her. (Job 31:5–8, 10)

Whoa, mama! That is what you call the open-kimono prayer. The dude is naked before God because he wants

God's man prays the brave prayers of continual growth.

growth and spiritual integrity. It's a bring-it-on confession and prayer. Key words: "Let God weigh me." Are you willing to go there in your walk with God? The place of full examination? If so, you will experience His dream and catch His vision for your life.

What will be the results if you keep moving your borders of growth?

- new insights
- less selfish impulse
- new character
- less confusion
- new conduct
- less confession
- new spirit
- less collateral damage
- new growth
- less disappointment
- more impact
- less regret
- more motivation
- less frustration

No extra charge for the deep, gasping adrenaline rushes and unforgettable testimonies of God's power, which will also be yours. Read that list again. Go ahead. God says, *That's what I want for you.*

Paddling into DREAM

In my last book, *Risk,* I challenged God's men around the world to take stock of their faith and let God be big—really big. If God is allowed to be who He says He is, then we will make equally big choices that please God and help others. In *Dream,* it's about becoming a great man who seeks glory by joining God's personal process of becoming like His Son, leaving fantasies of greatness, and choosing to embrace our everyday reality to bring Him glory. To become God's man, you will **D**ecide to let God decide for you, **R**eside in the glory of your reality, **E**xchange your vision for God's, **A**ccept God's process, and **M**ove your borders in continual growth.

As you read, watch for the big wave rider image. When you get to each one, a place of application, that's your signal to stop, pray, and reflect on a spiritual principle for realizing God's vision. In the chapters ahead, you'll find that the essence of living the dream as God's man is letting God decide who you are and learning to apply what He shows you. The goals are simple, yet all require faith.

So…*connect* with God's vision for your life, *cooperate* with what God reveals, and *create* new relationships that bring Him glory.

Ready to hit the surf? Paddle out, my brother.

chapter 2

leaking Jesus

People often use the phrase "like father, like son" to refer to
family resemblance. When people see my likeness in my kids,
it pleases me. God wants his children to bear his image and
likeness, too.

—Dr. Rick Warren

I don't know if you've noticed, but babies leak.

They also require close proximity. At times this is a lethal combination
for any parent, aunt, uncle, brother, or sister who happens to be holding
one when they—hmm, how can I put this delicately?—you know,
leak. What's inside comes out and onto those unfortunate enough to be
in the hot zone. Smells, drools, and foods, and don't forget those happy
numbers one and two. I think maybe God designed it this way to show
us exactly how big His love is for us and how it works. His precious and
wonderful creations that make messes. Out of His love, He cleans up and
cleans up until we grow up. This is grace.

My daughter Cara leaked on me when she was two. It happened exactly as you might expect. I was in her hot zone as she was sitting happily on

my lap. An electrical signal made its way from Cara's cerebral cortex to her bladder as she nested contentedly with me at a party. That neurobiological event transpired while I was deeply engaged in a real life 911 story being told by my friend Jeff, a fire captain. As designed, Cara's bladder received the transmission, unlocked, and unleashed the fluid which should have been captured and contained by parental countermeasures.

But for a flawed connection. The diaper tape that holds the material in the proper position had come loose. A small and unnoticeable shift in diaper alignment was now leading to a major diaper breach. The mighty Mississippi was about to overwhelm a broken levy.

At the same time, an electrical signal made its way to my brain to notice that something was happening in the lower regions. Unexpected, this notice took a little while to translate. The first signal—the warm sensation on my right quadricep—was flatly rejected. The phone was ringing, but I let the answering machine pick up. More warming on the leg—another notice. This time the signal was reinforced by an unmistakable aroma. A surprise attack of overwhelming baby fluids. It was a potty Pearl Harbor—Cara the Japanese, and I the unsuspecting Pacific Fleet. Recognition and response were simply too late. The bombs were away, and I was sleeping below deck. So what did I do? I scrambled for the bathroom like a bomb-squad flunky, through the crowd, holding the bomb away from my body in case of any remaining contamination. Of course, you guessed it—not a drop was left. The evacuation to the bathroom only resulted in a gleeful smile on Cara, as if realizing what fun she had caused.

In life, what's inside will eventually come out. And there's nothing you can do to stop it. We do our best to prevent spills and leaks. Diapers, Tupperware, and window caulking all prevent undesirable seepage of stuff into the protected spaces of our lives. But when it comes to our character—the stuff inside that guides critical decision making— there are no controls to stop the leaks. And frequently, we leak onto others.

It goes like this: Signals and stimuli inevitably trigger a flood of your character, which spills into your everyday interactions. These spills have a shaping influence on those around us. Jesus put it this way: "The good man brings good things out of the good stored up in him, and the evil man brings evil things out of the evil stored up in him" (Matthew 12:35).

The big question is, what sort of character are you leaking?

Diapers and Destiny

Okay, man, you with me here? I should probably apologize for that graphic analogy, but it's memorable, don't you think? What's inside must come out.

Let's translate the simple progression of my leaking episode with Cara into some basic parallels to our characters as God's men.

- *Acceptance.* The physical processes in babies are accepted and inevitable. What's happening in us emotionally, relationally, morally, and spiritually will come out and influence the lives of others. Both are unstoppable, organic human processes designed by God.
- *Proximity.* In both settings, physical proximity determines the blast zone of influence. Having Cara in my lap put me in her hot zone. Spouses, kids, friends, and co-workers are in your hot zone of character and conduct.
- *Activation.* Once filled, a baby's bladder is signaled to unload. It can't not give way. When you connect with people, your character can't not give way to conduct. One is a fluid that gets eliminated as waste, but the other is your character expressed in behavior that has an ongoing influence.
- *Sensation.* A diaper expands, gets heavy, starts to smell—and my leg and Cara's shorts get wet. Over time, the people connected to you sense and feel the real you. Our dignity gets pulled away, and they get a whiff of what's inside.
- *Saturation.* There's a transfer that takes place. From body to diaper to pants to leg! Leaking substances land somewhere; they seep into things and change their makeup. Clean becomes dirty. Similarly, any fears, pride, insecurities, brokenness, attachments, or wounds can seep into our relationships and change them for better or for worse.
- *Recognition and reaction.* With Cara, I didn't notice what was happening right away. And when I finally did, it was too late. The same is true in the hot zone of male character, both positive and negative. Unfortunately, it's often negative. Pick up the newspapers for a study in the sociology of male choice effervescing out of male character onto others. You will see an epidemic of personal diseases, fatherlessness, family disintegration, and pain. The devastated will tell you there was often no time to mitigate the disaster until it was too late.

It seems like my sin and character flaws leak more aggressively than the healthier parts of me. I hate it when those parts of me win. Just the other day, my best strength became my flaw. The result: I leaked the bad stuff onto my whole family.

Leaking Self

"Welcome to Taco Bell; may I take your order?"

We had worked through the order as we sat in the drive-through line. Or so I thought. I hit the window button, stuck my head out, and responded with, "I need three cheesy gordita crunches, two crunchwrap supremes and three bean burritos with no onion." Phew. What an ordeal! In our family, drive-through orders are fraught with the roadside bombs of last-minute changes. I try to get the ordering escrow done before the pressure of the line of cars behind me and the microphone in front of me apply the crunch.

This time I was ready.

But as I was delivering the order from the car committee to the Taco Bell senate, a voice of dissent suddenly rose from the representative seated next to me.

"I don't want a cheesy gordita crunch," my wife, Chrissy, said.

Uh-oh.

I paused and listened to the microphone repeat back to me, "That's three cheesy gordita crunches, two crunchwrap…"

A second appeal from Chrissy started simultaneously, this time with more energy and the unmistakable tone. You know, *that* tone? It's used when

> *"Welcome to Taco Bell; may I take your order?"*

the speaker is not representing the group as he should and ignoring the proper procedure for correction.

Oh, boy. Excellent listener that I am, I pressed on and replied, "That's right."

"Your total will be ten forty-five at the window." I took my foot off the brake and nudged five feet forward. There were two cars ahead of us.

"I don't want a cheesy gordita crunch," Chrissy repeated. The tone had intensified. Of course, it was justified—I blew her off under the pressure of the line behind. I reasoned that I would surrender my crunchwrap for her cheesy gordita and everybody would be satisfied. The recourse made, relief ensued.

But then I pounced, leaking ridicule of Chrissy's untimely switch. I made fun of her tone, her drama, the catharsis of the cheesy crunch fiasco that had been so simply defused. In fact, the whole family piled on and we had a nice, big laugh at her expense—my Chrissy, who is not thin-skinned, laughed along at herself.

The hazing should have died there. But it didn't.

The next night, my kids decided to replay the Taco Bell incident to my in-laws and nephew while we sat at their dinner table. Somehow, it wasn't so funny the second time. Especially to Chrissy. It was open season on Mommy, and it went on, and on, and didn't stop. Other embarrassing stuff came up, too, as the escalation continued. And still I didn't protect her. Even Jenna, my little princess, jumped into the feeding frenzy. Finally, sensing there was too much mommy chum in the water, I half-heartedly tried to redirect the conversation, but my protection came too late. I flashed a look at the kids, but the damage was already done. I dismissed myself to gather our things and retreated to join my son upstairs. When we finally got to the car, the consequences of my leak came out in a flood. I was forced to accept that I was the source of the negative emotions boiling inside my wife. As the leader of our family, it was my responsibility to step in, and I had let it get out of control, and then had done very little to stop it. I hate it when I am the source.

Two hours later, our whole family sat in the living room and apologized to Chrissy for how we treated her. Our family (thanks to me) can be highly competitive, which is okay in some contexts. But it's bad when it comes to relationships. This side of my character comes out when we sense an advantage or there's a laugh to be had. Most of the time, as a family, we can laugh at ourselves or each other without crossing the line and cutting someone to shreds. But this time, competition led to oppression which led to humiliation which led to a significant attack, beyond disrespect and straight on to a verbal assault. One member of the family had stopped laughing and started hurting and no one had noticed. Like punching a soft bruise, each blow stopped being funny and started tearing at the emotional flesh of someone we love.

I asked the family if we were proud of what we'd done that night, if honor described how we treated Chrissy. There was a moment of silence, and then, with tears rolling down our faces, we all agreed: absolutely not. I was ashamed that I leaked that part of my character onto my family and allowed competition to lead to oppression. Chrissy was willing to laugh at herself in the drive-through, but she had no reason to expect it to become a litany of public abuse. We all stood back, took inventory, apologized, and sought her forgiveness. What was inside of us blasted out and severed our fellowship with the most loving, gracious, and respectable person in the family.

In my family it is known as the Taco Bell torture episode: a real low point in the history of Luck relationships. And the object was my wife. Maybe your family is different, but in our home we tend to take the mom for granted—a lot. She is the proverbial glue that makes everything work. Were she a CEO, she would be throwing down six figures dealing with all the management particulars and needs in our family of five. Chrissy makes it so easy for me to sweep in on my silver jetpack and be the hero in our family because she is in the jungle clearing away the brush for me to land every day. Let's put it this way: it's not easy being her, but she accepts her responsibilities willingly and without resentment, making sacrifices for us without the appreciation she deserves. She is God's woman. I say this with a grimace on my face, but I made God's woman snap, and it all started in a Taco Bell drive-through.

> **dream fact**
> *Our human weaknesses provide occasions for the triumph of divine power.*

Character influences those around us in profound and sometimes imperceptible ways. Competitive and aggressive DNA can be a good quality for kids facing obstacles. But in relationships, it's better to connect than compete. Outside of the Holy Spirit's control, my greatest gifts and strengths become my greatest weaknesses.

We can't stop the leaking, but God's dream changes what's coming out. In short, He prefers the water main of His character to transform our stink into a new, pleasing expression. He wants to replace the leaking sin and selfishness with the redeeming character of Christ.

The titanic irony is that our human weaknesses provide occasions for the triumph of divine power. It did that night in my family, and it will in your life when you understand exactly what God's dream is: that you leak Jesus more and leak self less. One expression of character makes healthy relationships. The other produces harm. One makes you better. The other makes messes. One involves surrender. The other involves slavery. One brings love, sacrifice, and salvation to a dying world. The other brings disconnection and destruction.

God's dream for us is to create more attraction to Him and less cynicism about Christianity:

> But thanks be to God, who always leads us in triumphal procession in Christ and *through us spreads everywhere the fragrance of the knowledge of him. For we are to God the aroma of Christ* among those who are being saved and those who are perishing. To the one *we are the smell of death; to the other, the fragrance of life.* And who is equal to such a task? Unlike so many, we do not peddle the word of God for profit. On the contrary, in Christ we speak before God with sincerity, like men sent from God." (2 Corinthians 2:14–17)

This is the smell of God's man.

Take a Whiff

Visibility. Identity. Usability. Portability. Eternity. Availability. Integrity.

These words describe God's aggressive strategy for leaking heaven all over the earth through you. Each word is realized in every God's man as he increasingly surrenders his life to Jesus Christ and the influence of the Holy Spirit. Not only does this dream of God satisfy our deepest longings for significance, it leads us to where the real glory resides—people seeing and experiencing Jesus in you.

Visibility

"But thanks be to God, who always leads us in triumphal procession." That, my friend, is what we call a good old-fashioned victory parade. Picture a Roman general proudly leading his troops in a victory procession while the people applaud and cheer in the streets. Who said God doesn't like visibility of His guys? He wants you noticed. He wants your victories acknowledged. He wants others to see the new you created in Christ who is doing good works. He wants you to be totally identified with Him, His fields of battle in the world, and His total defeat of the Enemy. Why? Because your victories give Him glory.

Identity

Two words make sense of all this visibility—"in Christ." The victory procession is led by the Captain of salvation. Who will the people identify as the hero? Christ. Who will be credited as the orchestrator of those victories in your life? Christ. Who is the one that inspired you to fight by sacrificing His life for yours? Christ. Whose character in you defeated sin in your life? Christ's. Who is the One who rescued you from defeat? Christ. Who gave you a new purpose? Christ. He receives these accolades and you share in His glory. God's dream for me is that my visibility on earth comes about through my identity in Christ precisely because that is the only kind of visibility that brings glory to Him. It is not a self-serving visibility that pads my insecurities. It is a Christ-honoring visibility that shows

> **dream fact**
> *Christ gave you a new purpose.*

itself in my actions for Him. I am His trophy.

Usability

"And through us…" It is one thing to be associated with greatness, but to be engaged proactively in building something great with Christ is a long way for a sinner to travel. The sinner's dream is to be delivered from his sin. God takes the dream light years beyond that by electing to use the sinner as a vessel to pour out hope and salvation onto those around him. The phrase "through us" shows Jesus connected with us in a task. The emphasis, when placed on the "us," carries with it that sense of disbelief that this man is allowed to do this great work. People say, "What? Who, him? With Him?" Pure shock and awe.

Portability

"Spreads everywhere the fragrance of the knowledge of him." This is the genius of God's plan: everywhere God's man goes, the message goes. Everywhere means everywhere. It doesn't matter where you live, work, travel, or play, you have two jobs when people are present. If you are with Christians, your job is to leak Jesus through edification—to build them up and strengthen their faith in Christ. If you are with non-Christians, your purpose is to leak Jesus for evangelization—to win them to Christ. Wherever you go, you leak, and people are reached for God's purposes.

Eternity

"For we are to God the aroma of Christ among those who are being saved and those who are perishing. To the one we are the smell of death; to the other, the fragrance of life." Our job is to smell, not judge how others react to our smell. The Jesus aroma released by God's man is always sweet smelling, even though it may be rejected more than it is accepted. That's why it takes guts to follow Christ—many men will reject His invitation to come. Our faithfulness is the only basis of evaluation, not how many we influence.

Availability and Integrity

"And who is equal to such a task? Unlike so many, we do not peddle the word of God for profit. On the contrary, in Christ we speak before God with sincerity, like men sent from God." Read that one back slowly. Can you swallow it? Does that verse describe who you want to be? Are you a man who is willing to accept "such a task"? To let Christ glorify Himself through you in a powerful way, you need availability and sincerity. Availability is an easy one. That simply has to do with your willingness to become like Christ! But alongside your willingness there must be integrity. As Paul points out to his readers, "so many" use God for selfish purposes rather than allowing God to use their lives for His purposes. Somewhere along the line there's a pollution of purpose. Their identity and activity for God are at cross purposes with their integrity. These men cannot be used greatly. Something is wrong in their character. They have not allowed Christ to penetrate fully into the depths of their lives. They are compartmentalized in their character or "dis-integrated" on the inside. Parts of these men are not totally comfortable with truth and reality, and they serve the Lord with mixed motives and unhealthy character. Behind the mask of their Christianity, they are asking "What's in it for me?" They are peddlers, pimping Christ for their own gain. They have lost that accountability and awareness of God's presence to guide them. You cannot trust them. Why? They lack spiritual integrity. By contrast, sincere men of God are welcomed to apply. These are the "on the contrary" squad men wide open to God's leadership, methods, directions, and decisions over their own. More specifically, they consistently choose those directions and methods that will give Christ the most glory in their lives.

Owning the Family Resemblance

By now, I trust you are resolved as God's man to allow the character of Jesus Christ to leak out of you and into your spheres of influence. This is God's dream for you—to bear His likeness. The rest of our journey in *Dream* is going to center on the character of Christ, so we can accommodate more of it in our own lives through faith and in partnership with the Holy Spirit. I pray that as you move forward, you would do it in a spirit of partnership with the Holy Spirit. How do you do that? Simply ask for Him to reveal, convict, and lead you through His promptings, leadings, revelations, and, more important, your circumstances that clearly call you out and welcome Christ in. You might want to pause and do this right now. Go ahead.

It helps to know that the Holy Spirit is not failing in your life and will reveal to you the areas where your character is out of alignment, where it needs a tune-up or a full-on overhaul. These moments will be uncomfortable, then worthwhile, and finally invaluable as you join increasingly in God's dream for you to become like His Son—to own a family resemblance which pleases Him.

No matter where you are in your spiritual journey, study the life of Jesus to imitate how He interacts with people. In the end, your goal is new character expressed in new conduct that impacts people and brings new life. Many times, having this effect will involve sacrificing something that is a part of you in order to gain Christ. This may mean a new way of looking at people, a new way of thinking, a new way of acting and inter-acting, and a new way of reaching out to others. In all these, a cost comes with the benefit. The full dream is that we would be willing to sacrifice it all—to be crucified with Christ in order to point others to Him.

God forms His Son into our lives in ways we would not always choose ourselves. God's men through the ages recognized that suffering was part of the process if the dream was to be accomplished. "We always carry around in our body the death of Jesus," Paul wrote, "so that the life of

> *God forms His Son into our lives in ways we would not always choose ourselves.*

Jesus may also be revealed in our body. For we who are alive are always being given over to death for Jesus' sake, so that his life may be revealed in our mortal body. So then, death is at work in us, but life is at work in you" (2 Corinthians 4:10–12). The point is this: sacrifices and suffering are part of the deal. What will those sacrifices look like for you? Only God knows. So if you are reading this and are experiencing a trial that is stretching you to the limit—be encouraged, my brother. Because like a blacksmith forging tempered steel, God is forging His Son in you.

If you are tempted to grab a parachute and bail out of the dream, or if you are asking God if there is another way "to do this thing," you are in good company. In the end, I am praying that you will pray as he prayed at that moment: "Father, if you are willing, take this cup from me; yet not my will, but yours be done" (Luke 22:42). Jesus was honest with God about the difficulty of accepting the plan. It was not going to feel good at all. He prayed for another way. But He was surrendered to God. In the end, Jesus wanted God's plan more than His own comfort. That's a gutsy man praying a gutsy prayer.

What does it take to become like our leader Jesus? Total submission to let God direct the dream of Christlikeness, giving Him unrestricted freedom to choose the way to accomplish it.

In the chapters that follow, we will take a quality of Christ and explore how it is expressed. We'll flesh out what it means by looking at real men who crossed over from the likeness of man to the likeness of the Son of Man. Our goal is this: "And we, who with unveiled faces all reflect the Lord's glory, are being transformed into his likeness with *ever-increasing glory*, which comes from the Lord, who is the Spirit" (2 Corinthians 3:18). This dream is an ever-increasing process over a lifetime. Like me, you will get loose in the corners of your character from time to time. You can count on it. The key is that when those moments of revelation come, when you see the gaps between you and Christ, see them as coming from God to make you like Christ. Have faith in His dream for you.

Now, my brother, it's time to look at what you're leaking and what Christ was leaking.

chapter 3

no neon

The sufficiency of my own merit is to know that my merit is
not sufficient.

—AUGUSTINE

The melody was familiar, but the language was foreign.

I stood in a twenty-by-fifty-foot wooden shack in the mountainous
region of southern Mexico. A small boy with soiled clothes and face
stood to my left, looking up at the very tall white man as his mother and
other Tzotsil (pronounced SOAT-sil) women crashed tambourines and
danced in unison in front of the congregation. I was caught in a holy
haze, a cacophony of sights and sounds. Bass notes and acoustic noises
coalesced with their ancient Mayan dialect to make a spiritual declaration
in song. It was like watching *Apocalypto* without the subtitles. (Tzotsil is
a dialect of the Yucatan Mayan spoken in Gibson's film.) I googled my
brain for a melody match and got a hit twenty seconds later. Then as the
next chorus flooded the shack, there was no doubt. My soul now began
to play the audio file and my lips joined in:

"I have decided…to follow Jesus… I have decided to follow Jesus… I have decided to follow Jesus… No turning back…no turning back." My singing in English. The others singing in their native tongue. Tears began to flow, my arms were raised, and the sweet embrace of the Holy Spirit saturated every cell of my body. Cognitively, I did not understand a thing. Spiritually, this was a burning bush experience. This shack was consumed by the presence of God, and we were all still standing. Like Moses, I was afraid to open my eyes.

Just twenty minutes earlier, I was standing outside this shack listening to the pastor tell the story of how the church was planted. In matter-of-fact language, he explained that local tribal leaders kicked the snot out of him on this very spot. He asked for it. Pastor Refugio (pronounced reh-FEW-gee-oh), along with a host of other Tzotsil Indians in his village, left ritual Mayan paganism for a new way—the Jesus way. This did not sit well with the local caciques (pronounced kah-SEE-kays), or bosses who maintain cultural homogeny and enforce it viciously when people stray.

Decades of the persecution of Refugio's people is well documented in this region of Chiapas but goes unprosecuted, unnoticed by the outside world. The caciques especially hate pastors and like to make examples of them. Pastors are the source of their pain and the object of their anger. Every word that comes out of Refugio's mouth condemns him as a marked man. Our translator explained that Refugio's conversion, along with others in his village, has seriously hampered the cash flow for the mob bosses who control and extort locals who practice Mayan paganism. These "leaders" coerce the rural Indian families into purchasing the accessories connected to pagan rituals: sacrificial chickens, candles, and an alcoholic potion used in worship called posh. The caciques also require family celebrations that are funded by money loaned at exorbitant interest rates to financially trap poor villagers in financial prostitution. Bottom line: Christianity in this neck of the world is an unwelcome burr under the criminal saddle. And while the persecution of Christians is done in the name of culture, it's the bottom line that drives it. This realization came together for me before the translator finished the story.

The story played like the Mexican version of *The Godfather.* The caciques put out a contract on Refugio. First they beat him up and told him to shut up or else. When that didn't work, the caciques set out to eliminate God's man. No more warnings. This time fists are replaced with shot-

> *The story played like the Mexican version of* **The Godfather.**

guns. The translator described an old-fashioned assassination—a mark, a group of hit men, and a preplanned moment in time for a kill shot. On a dark night the assassins surrounded Pastor Refugio's house and knocked on his door. He had thought a day like this would come, and he readied himself to die for Christ.

Then, according to Refugio and the newly converted assassin standing in front of me, a wind came audibly and visibly down the mountain and drew a line between the wolves and their prey. It was an unnatural wind that turned into a violent presence. The converted assassin describes the wind appearing like an eagle spreading its wings over them and causing them all to drop to the ground then flee. In short, Refugio survived, and out of the aborted assassination a church is born:

Alas de Aguila: Wings of Eagles.

I looked at the ground. I looked at the shack with its small white sign, an eagle painted in blue. I looked at the converted assassin. I looked at the surrounding village in the middle of nowhere. I absorbed the picture of poverty surrounding me. I smelled the heavy burnt air that engulfed this village. I looked at this little man—five foot nothing, a hundred and nothing pounds—and began feeling very small. It hit me that he walks home every day down this rural road under threat of his life. It unnerved me that very few people will ever see or know his bravery. It killed me that I get to go, and he must stay and live out his faith under such stressful conditions. I looked at his one pig, his one-room house, and his wife and five little ones. *This place I am standing on is holy ground,* I thought. It was the burning bush of Exodus here in Chiapas. A people engulfed in the flames of persecution but not burning up because God's hand is on a man, walking with him amidst the flames.

I grabbed Pastor Refugio by both shoulders and turned his face toward mine. There was something I had to tell him. I looked into his face and said in Spanish, "I want you to know that you have a brother in America who will be standing with you in prayer. I want you to know that my family will pray for you and your family. I want you to know that you will never be forgotten. You will be on our hearts and in our minds." I had nothing else to offer.

His eyes began to swell with tears. No one but he alone was able to carry Refugio's cross day to day. But for that moment in time, it felt like this warrior sensed a halo of safety in which to let his guard down and just be a man. Through tears he told me of his burdens, his fears for his family, and how he felt so isolated. But just when I thought he was breaking down, he raised an arm, defiantly pointed to his modest shack of a church, and began sharing his hopes for a bigger building. He fanned his arm over the space where it would reside, telling me the decisive details. He told me how the same mighty God who came to protect him on the night of death with wings like an eagle's will accomplish this vision. He was full of faith, not shrinking from his God-appointed mission to labor in obscurity—this mission he proudly accepted.

Pastor Refugio is a giant of the faith. *How does he earn that label?* you ask. One word—*humility.*

Getting to know Refugio, I saw that his greatness was not a measure of how God used him but his response to how God chose to use him. Press the Rewind button and you will see a man content to be a pawn in a grander plan. You will see a man cooperating with God in the role God wanted him to play. You witness a spirit that is content to live in the background, backwoods, and hostile back countries of the kingdom. No rebellion. No retreat. Just coop-eration with God. Go figure: they send the brute squad, beat him bloody, and leave him lying in the dirt with a little time to rethink his position.

> **dream fact**
> *To be humble and dedicated day in and day out is the stuff of God's men.*

Imagine you are Refugio. *Hmm. Option A: I'm out of here! Option B: Don't be so obvious. Option C: Stay, build a church, and jump back in the ring for more.*

See, he's not in it for himself. Refugio has disappeared. He's in this for God and for people who need Him. He doesn't need titles or position or safety to maintain his dignity. He doesn't care if he gets some credit or any credit as long as the kingdom work is being done. He doesn't barter with or try to manipulate God. Nope. Instead, in a spirit of brokenness and dependence upon God, he rests in God's sovereignty, humbly recognizing that he might have to wait until he's taken to heaven before any of God's promises are fulfilled through his suffering. His humility on earth comes from eternal ambition, a low estimation of his own importance in light of more eternal ambitions and assurances. He's got nothing to prove to the thugs. He's been the recipient of so much generosity from God that his pride and fear are no match for his humility and courage.

To be the man that Refugio is day in and day out is the stuff of God's men:

- disciplined inner strength
- God-centered power
- aggressive pursuit
- bold initiative
- sacrificial for a great cause
- delayed gratification
- rising in the face of intimidation
- eternal ambition

Content and secure in the Father means humble in the most aggressive sense. When a man is declared to be important by God and his mission is approved by God, he is free to be humble.

- nothing to prove
- content with self
- desiring recognition from God alone
- trusting God with your station in life
- not threatening
- at ease with the weak

- easy to embrace
- no need to get the credit
- not in competition

Without this emotional posture, Refugio's circumstances would hinder his freedom to be so disciplined and spiritually aggressive. True humility breeds the virtues of his masculinity. The result? The little giant from Chiapas is living the dream every God's man feels deeply in the magma of his soul: to act nobly and humbly before God and man.

This is the dance that few men are able to pull off. Most attempt to do it without Christ. He is either missing from their recipe or dysfunctionally blended in so that He can never quite be seen or felt. These men never fully realize the dream of greatness or develop into the men they crave to be. The unredeemed elements of pride and fear prevail over the spirit of Christ. The result: their dream of greatness is dead.

That is why God's man, like Refugio, needs to have a confident grip of God in his life. When we are disconnected from a clear understanding of God's abilities, God's love, God's attitude toward us, and God's dream for us, we simply cannot let go of these hindrances:

- the need to be noticed
- the need to prove our worth
- images
- the need to be first
- trying to please people
- self
- prejudice
- hurts

In the simplest form, we cannot experience and develop Christlike humility and experience God's dream for our lives. But if we remain humble enough to see Him clearly, we will know and experience a new level of vision and service from the inside out.

Humility is at the heart of adopting Jesus's character because it is at the heart of redemption. That means we need to learn how to wear our influence.

Royalty Without a Crown

Jesus did not need neon.

The humble King is an oxymoron unless you are talking about Christ. Noble and self-effacing. Powerful and gentle. Authoritative and accepting. Sovereign yet submitted. Royal yet humble. Yep, this is our man. We are called to imitate, model, and project the ability to temper our influence with humility for God's purposes in others. To do this we need to think humbly.

dream fact
Jesus did not need neon.

Think of yourselves the way Christ Jesus thought of himself. He had equal status with God but didn't think so much of himself that he had to cling to the advantages of that status no matter what. Not at all. When the time came, he set aside the privileges of deity and took on the status of a slave, became human! Having become human, he stayed human. It was an incredibly humbling process. He didn't claim special privileges. Instead, he lived a selfless, obedient life and then died a selfless, obedient death—and the worst kind of death at that—a crucifixion. Because of that obedience, God lifted him high and honored him far beyond anyone or anything, ever, so that all created beings in heaven and on earth—even those long ago dead and buried—will bow in worship before this Jesus Christ, and call out in praise that he is the Master of all, to the glorious honor of God the Father. (Philippians 2:5–11, MSG)

God's dream for you looks like this:

- You have influence without ego.
- You are capable of retaliation but choose reconciliation.
- You pass up power to increase God's influence.
- You submit to God's plans versus presuming them.
- You freely notice others.
- You empty yourself instead of being self-entitled.
- You are willing to take the hit in humble obedience to God's purposes.
- You are able to wait for God to honor your efforts in His time.

That's God's dream for you because that is Jesus—the likeness He created you to reflect and reveal.

So, Kenny, how do I apply this?

There are a ton of possible responses, but I believe a God's man says to himself, *I want to carry myself like that during my mission on earth.* Ask yourself:

- *Do I see Jesus's humility clearly?*
- *Do I want this character quality of Jesus in my own life?*

- *What sort of character do people sense when they're around me? Do I make things easier or harder for them by being humble?*
- *Am I at ease among the marginalized of society or people not like me?*
- *Am I stand-offish or easily embraced by others?*

After you answer these questions with an honest assessment, take the first step of humility by submitting your life to Christ (again, if you have to). Tell Him you want to be like Him, ask Him to help you depend on Him, so that you can learn to be humble and think humbly. Practically, this means that under God's control, we exchange, as Jesus did:

- comfort for discomfort
- flattery for faithfulness
- status for service
- harshness for graciousness
- titles for treasures in heaven
- safety for suffering

That's what Jesus-style humility looks like. That's what it means to be humbly significant.

Jesus Says, "Chillax!"

In California we invent language. Our lexicon is free spirited and laid-back, if you know what I mean…dude. If there were a gifted program in our schools for language creation, my son would be in it. Don't ask me why he is not satisfied with regular words. Like many native Californians, he's a linguistic bohemian, and his use of word creations is nonstop. Lately, he's been using an amalgam of "chill" and "relax"—"chillax." Can you feel it? Whereas "chill" can carry negative connotations, as in "Would you just chill out?" and "relax" isn't strong enough, this little expression is picking up momentum. It's become a highly contagious linguistic virus spreading across the country. The best thing about the word *chillax* is that there is an instant emotional connection. Just saying it makes me calm down on the inside and let my burdens go.

The axis of humility is internal. It is an emotional posture that makes the people in your presence feel unburdened, light, and connected to you all at the same time. Your presentation is unforced but strong. This is because, at its roots, true Christ-based humility in a man combines a modest opinion of one's own importance with an excessively high estimation of the importance of God and people. In a personal encounter, the possessor of humility disappears as an

dream fact
Jesus was especially good at speaking the language of calm.

emotional obstacle to the other person and leaves two powerful forces in their place: God's presence and the other person's importance. Think Jesus and prostitute. Feel the interaction between Jesus and the woman at the well. Revisit Jesus and the lepers. Reread about Jesus and the man born blind. What did they all experience? They all stood in God's presence and felt safe and connected to God. Humbling, isn't it?

To the lonely, marginalized, burdened, stressed, or frenzied, a humble God's man is who they need. That is why Jesus so liberally offered His humility to us—it is refreshing! "Come to me, all you who are weary and burdened, and I will give you rest. Take my yoke upon you and learn from me, *for I am gentle and humble in heart,* and you will find rest for your souls. For my yoke is easy and my burden is light" (Matthew 11:28–30). The message is:

- "Just take a deep breath."
- "Everything is going to be all right."
- "I am safe."
- "I will not abuse your trust."
- "I'll show you how."
- "Walk with me."
- "You will feel freer and better."

From Jesus's perspective, His offer is attractive not because of the promise or the result. In His mind, you accept His invitation because you see and want His character. You let Jesus into your life and let Him show you how to manage it because you know He will not harm you. He is "gentle and humble in heart," and because we know this, we keep coming back. Ultimately, knowing Him brings us to a place of trust where we can unload what's happening inside of us. His humility produces vulnerability which is reexpressed in our own humble acceptance of His offer. His availability and ability are pluses, but His humility creates that safety to come. Jesus was especially good at speaking the language of calm.

Jesus knows that we need to chillax, and He invites us to pause and possess peace. His humility converts our anxiety to tranquility. In Him, we find rest.

So have you humbly accepted Jesus's invitation? Do you allow His character to expand your ability to trust and obey? Do you exchange your yoke for His and let Him show you the ropes? Do you learn from Him?

The first step to developing Christlike humility is humbly unburdening yourself to Christ. You cannot possess Christ unless you are willing to risk humble surrender to Him. Jesus liked the show-how method of developing humility. Take a look back at his words from Matthew:

- I do; you watch.
- I do; you participate.
- We do it together.
- You do; I watch.

This is the invitation to the "humblee" (you) to have a relationship with your "Humbler." God and man, Savior and sinner, Brother-King and servant join to learn to become like Him.

Humble Pie, Please

Jesus-style humility has personal influence under the control and management of the Holy Spirit. He whispers; *Stop talking about yourself and get interested in who God is!* He invites you to take some of that bonus you just got and give it to that inner-city ministry you've been thinking about. He moves you to connect with that neighbor—the single mom with a son—by inviting her boy to go with your family to the big game this Saturday. Are you feeling it? Humility before God manifests itself in controlling your ability to influence. The trouble comes when we transfer that control to a feeling, the moment, convenience, a fear, or our appetites. Each of us has influence, and we'll project that onto others for better or for worse. The question is, how will you use yours?

Will you be the dad who uses his position to intimidate, demand, and threaten? Or will you be the man in the family who leads out of service more than position? Will you be the man who possesses wealth for his own pleasure? Or will you be the man who gives God control of your finances for His pleasure? Will you be the man who says, *I deserve better than this*? Or will you be God's man who says, *I'm willing to wait for Your timing on this one, Lord*? The languages of entitlement, conditions, and selfishness are not spoken in the land of humility. They are foreign tongues that make sense only to those men given first to pride—masking their fears of being truly great by wasting their influence and affluence upon themselves. God says, *Come to Me and I will give you something more permanent—greatness and glory in being like My Son. Come to Me and learn from Me. You will achieve a greatness that touches others powerfully.*

The lens of Jesus's mission on earth was humility—that's where it had to start. He had to balance His divinity and His ministry to men. He had to manage His capacity to influence and His Father's purpose for Him. He had to learn the rhythm of possessing royalty without flaunting His crown. You may not be a celebrity, but you have influence. Similarly, you may not be pulling down six figures, but I know you have relational capital in the lives of others. For God's man, greatness on earth starts with humble surrender—giving yourself to Christ and refusing to resist His power. Everybody starts there. "Humble yourselves, therefore, under God's mighty hand, that he may lift you up in due time" (1 Peter 5:6).

dream fact
We have to get on our face to see His face.

We have to get on our face to see His face. We have to get low in our estimation of ourselves to get high in God's estimation of us. We have to reflect humility to reveal Christ on earth. When we take this step, we are able to do more for God and people than we ever dreamed—just like the King.

For more information on ministry to the persecuted church, go to the Open Doors USA Web site at www.odusa.org.

chapter 4

not so with you

Be ashamed to die until you have won some victory for
humanity.

—HORACE MANN

Fifty men were headed to the streets of Compton, Watts, and Harbor
City in South Central Los Angeles. There was a tangible excitement
as we circled together, prayed, loaded up our cargo, and headed north-
bound on Highway 5. Assisted by some great local pastors, we were
on a mission to find, help, and encourage single mothers. Each car was
loaded with large gift baskets filled with gift cards, chocolates, candles,
body products, CDs, school supplies, books, a Bible, gourmet meal kits,
and some other feminine things. The note card on each basket read,
On behalf of the local pastors in your community, a gift for you, and it
was signed by the sponsoring men's ministries. The actual face-to-face
presentations on the porches and doorsteps were a little different and
more personal.

Knock, knock, knock.

The door opened three inches, the chain still latched.

"Hi, my name is Doug, and we're here with Every Man Ministries. A pastor in the community gave us your name. We're here today to present this gift basket to you, pray with you, and just see if you need help with anything."

Now put yourself in the shoes of an African American single mom.

"Knock, Knock."

"Who's there?"

"Bunch of white guys."

"Bunch-of-white-guys who?"

"Bunch of white guys with a basket for you!"

The actual words spoken behind the door went something like this: "Mom, there's a bunch of white guys standing on the porch holding a big basket with lotsa ribbon. Should I let 'em in?"

Tracy opened the door reluctantly. I made the canned speech and explained why we were there. We presented her with a basket intended "just for her." Then I asked, as we had at every house, "Is there anything we can do for you while we're here?"

Looking down, she said, "Well, there is one thing. I think there's a dead cat in the crawl space under the house. The whole house is smelling from it. No one can get in there to get it out. The city guys came, and their guy couldn't fit, so they just gave up. Do you think—" This was as far as she got before we asked to see the crawl space.

> *"Mom, there's a bunch of white guys on the porch. Should I let 'em in?"*

Once there, we saw why the city animal control guy gave up so quickly. A power meter was stationed in front of the opening almost completely blocking access. Brick, small space, meter, then another small space, then brick again. We stood staring at it, trying to engineer a solution. A cat could fit. But a man? Huh-uh.

I pulled off my jacket anyway and began to wedge into the small space. I got my head and shoulder partway through. But that was it. The smell was awful. Two other guys gave it a whirl with similar results. Then Dennis stepped up, a determined look on his face, holding a trash bag in one hand. I didn't hold a lot of hope for my friend and went across the street to deliver another basket. Fifteen minutes later, I heard loud applause and a cheer crackle through the neighborhood. It was coming from Tracy's house.

Standing in the center of her front yard, grimy and smelling like a litter box, was Dennis.

While I was a gone, a crowd had gathered when Dennis managed to slip under the house. He emerged like a triumphant Roman gladiator, hoisting the white plastic garbage bag with one fist, a rigid feline silhouette inside, and raising the other fist in victory. We should have cast him in bronze on the spot. He looked left and right, bobbing in that "I'm the man" sort of way.

Tracy was crying. Dennis's act of service removed any doubt about our agenda. After that, she embraced us with her whole heart. We all gathered on Tracy's porch, thanked God for the small miracle, and prayed for her and her children. Every stench-free breath on that day would be a reminder to Tracy that God hears prayers, spoken and unspoken.

Porch after porch, awkward greeting after awkward greeting, crying mom after crying mom, doors kept opening. God's heart poured out on women in South Central who were desperately in need of some encouragement and affirmation from men. Being a mom in a financially strained situation is brutal. It's triple-dog hard when men go MIA. But when we ministered to those women, we were vicariously repenting for our brothers, men who had contributed to these ripples of pain. Most moms were overwhelmed by the baskets worth hundreds of dollars. Some just stood in shock while their kids jumped up and down, trying to see the contents. Others fell apart, crying on the porch. Many told us that we were the direct answer to their prayers that week. For one day, hugs from strangers, prayer, tears, and soul connections were common experiences.

Meaning is everything.

Call it what you want—significance, contribution, glory, value—it's what we are all after. We want our experiences to matter somehow, to factor in, to produce something redemptive—and do something that transcends daily life. Men seek out all sorts of experiences because we want to discover the deeper things.

To this profound and eternal truth, I feel obligated to add that the myriad ways men try to fill that need for meaning are almost comical. Can I get an amen? In fact, the more improbable, challenging, and potentially dangerous the opportunity, the more intrigued men become. That's why I knew I wouldn't have any trouble recruiting men from South Orange County to join me on the project in South Central Los Angeles.

White guys in Compton? *Sign me up!*

"True heroism," remarked Arthur Ashe, "is remarkably sober, very undramatic. It is not the urge to surpass all others at whatever the cost but the urge to serve others at whatever the cost." He would know. Arthur Ashe was to tennis in the modern era what Jackie Robinson was to Major League Baseball—a black man breaking into a white man's sport.

> *The more improbable, challenging, and potentially dangerous the opportunity, the more intrigued men become.*

Both men suffered and sacrificed for the rest of the African American athletes to follow in their huge footsteps. They did the dirty work, they endured the pain, and their presence secured the future of others. They are culture busters. They acted in the favor of others.

Someone has to break the mold. Someone has to go after the dead cat. Someone has to do what's needed. Someone has to make others feel valued.

The Servant God?

It's like man to want to be served. It's like the Son of Man to serve. It's like God's man to reflect the Son of Man.

> Jesus called them together and said, "You know that the rulers of the Gentiles lord it over them, and their high officials exercise authority

over them. Not so with you. Instead, whoever wants to become great among you must be your servant, and whoever wants to be first must be your slave—just as the Son of Man did not come to be served, but to serve, and to give his life as a ransom for many." (Matthew 20:25–28)

We could get lost in a lot of great theology on this, but for our purposes, there are six words we must focus on in this verse to get to this aspect of Christlikeness. They are "just as the Son of Man."

In the golden age of the NBA, also known as the Michael Jordan (M.J.) era, there was a television ad campaign built around M.J. and the dreams of little boys and basketball. The ads would show highlights of M.J.'s gravity defying moves, ending in one thing: the ball sailing, banking, or being slam-dunked through the net. The way he played, the way he shot the ball, and the way he dunked was new, innovative, and totally cool. He turned basketball on its head and brought a whole new level to a familiar game. He was to basketball what Superman is to superheroes, what Mickey Mouse is to Disneyland. The TV ads would alternate back and forth between M.J. and the dreamers. We would see his moves at the NBA level and then the kids' moves on the playground and the men on the driveway. Everyone wanted to "be like Mike." The guy was a freak show of athleticism. The sports marketers tapped our admiration, and the cash flowed in. What exactly did they tap?

- aspiration—our desire to be great
- inspiration—our need for a vision of greatness
- idolization—our need for an object of greatness
- imitation—our desire to duplicate the style or behavior of greatness

The disciples felt the same thing for Jesus. They aspired to be like Him. They saw Him in action. They made Him the object. But frequently, they skipped the last part—imitation. They replaced that with selfish ambition. They confused their greatness with what made Jesus great. They got into arguments and disagreements over who would be appointed to a cabinet position in the Jesus administration. Even though they watched Him heal the sick, serve the outcasts, and preach the kingdom, they weren't getting it. They attached themselves to the activity His service produced and not to Him. Position and power replaced service and sacrifice in their hearts, and it was time for a literal "come to Jesus" meeting.

The velvet of His grace was taken off for these conversations. The belt of truth needed to be applied to their spiritual fannies. If they wanted to be great, they needed get one thing straight: you are never greater than when you are acting in the favor of others.

Service Tips

Jesus placed more than a few roadside bombs in the disciples' minds to destabilize their dysfunctional thinking about glory and greatness. Jesus put his finger in the chest of the disciples. He made sure they were feeling Him.

- "For who is greater, the one who is at the table or the one who serves? Is it not the one who is at the table? But I am among you as one who serves" (Luke 22:27).

    Service tip: God's man gets up off his blessed assurance and serves.

- "The teachers of the law and the Pharisees sit in Moses' seat…. They tie up heavy loads and put them on men's shoulders, but they themselves are not willing to lift a finger to move them…. The greatest among you will be your servant. For whoever exalts himself will be humbled, and whoever humbles himself will be exalted" (Matthew 23:2, 4, 11–12).

    Service tip: Don't pimp God for personal recognition. Forget personal recognition and be willing to act in favor of others.

- "So he got up from the meal, took off his outer clothing, and wrapped a towel around his waist. After that, he poured water into a basin and began to wash his disciples' feet, drying them with the towel that was wrapped around him…. When he had finished washing their feet, he put on his clothes and returned to his place. 'Do you understand what I have done for you?' he asked them. 'You call me "Teacher" and "Lord" and rightly so, for that is what I am. Now that I, your Lord and Teacher, have washed your feet, you also should wash one another's feet. I have set you an example that you should do as I have done for you. I tell you the truth, no servant is greater than his master, nor is a messenger greater than the one who sent him. Now that you know these things, you will be blessed if you do them'" (John 13:4–5, 12–17).

    Service tip: If there is no act of service below the God-Man, there is certainly none below God's man.

I think after this they must have gotten the message. At Pentecost, His message and character coalesced in the baptism of the Holy Spirit, which began an explosion of service for God and people (see Acts 2–4).

In a man's world, authority and service often have an inverse relationship. The more authority, position, and power one possesses, the more that man is served. These guys get new titles and assistants, new offices and parking spots, and heaps of flattery and accommodation. In some cultures, men don't even need power or position to earn servitude. You simply have to be a man. The absence of higher

dream fact
True authority serves.

authority causes automatic deference to those with any power. It's called a pecking order.

In Jesus we see the opposite—the Authority served, and He preferred to do it in person. Watch Him in the Gospels. Study Him. He shows up, He counsels, He touches, He heals, He casts out demons, He mentors men, He encourages, He makes breakfast, He hugs the kids. Jesus breaks the rules to serve in person; He doesn't give money so that someone else can serve. His service was a sign that He was operating under a higher authority that freed Him to notice, lift up, and do what was needed in any given moment without consideration of man. He stood out dramatically because His contemporaries had abandoned their posts.

You follow the King who serves. His dream for you is to join Him.

> Teach us, good Lord, to serve as you deserve
> To give, and not count the cost,
> To fight, and not to heed the wounds,
> To toil, and not seek for rest,
> To labor, and not ask for reward,
> Save that of knowing that we do your will.

—Ignatius of Loyola

Relating to the Rascals

I like being with people who are like me. It's easier to be with like-minded people—comfortable and conflict free. But I've learned to also be energized by people outside my comfort zone. The Bible teaches that our inner circle of friends and advisors should be like-minded spiritually, but our focus on serving others should extend well past these borders. When you study the game film on Jesus, He is constantly breaking the rules that say whom He should be spending time with. Many times the disciples can't handle the freedom with which He moves and operates in His service. Jesus is not bound by culture. He is not tethered to the opinions of men. Instead, He's guided by compassion.

When it comes to whom you serve, the real test is not when you are with friends or family—it's when you are with "foreigners"—culturally, socially, or spiritually (although sometimes my own family seems foreign). In that sense, our King was countercultural. Let's see: women, kids, prostitutes, tax collectors, sinners, drunks, and lepers (to name a few) He honored with His presence, encouragement, and help. These were the people whom others threw money at but never sacrificed time or energy. Abraham Heschel said it this way in *A Passion for Truth,* "The test of love is in how one relates not to saints and scholars but to rascals." Jesus was definitely drawn to the rascals, and because He belonged only to God, He was freer than all the men around Him to engage and connect with "those people." He was free to serve exactly because He was a slave to all. He could forsake food, abandon cultural taboos, and stand tall

Christ transcends all barriers and unifies all people from all cultures.

against religiously motivated attacks because His primary identity was in the Father.

The apostle Paul was so much like Jesus in this sense. You can see Jesus leaking out of him as his identity in Christ frees him to be a slave to all. He is free to serve anyone from his duty to serve an audience of One. There are no borders to His service.

> Though I am free and belong to no man, I make myself a slave to everyone, to win as many as possible. To the Jews I became like a Jew, to win the Jews.... To the weak I became weak, to win the weak. I have become all things to all men so that by all possible means I might save some. (1 Corinthians 9:19–20, 22)

This is Paul's code of conduct as a servant of Christ—he belongs to all men as a servant because he belongs to Jesus. As there are no borders with nonbelievers, similarly, there are no borders between him and those he is called to serve. His passport is stamped by God alone as he exhorts God's people to remember their identity and act accordingly. He serves the body of Christ without barriers.

> Do not lie to each other, since you have taken off your old self with its practices and have put on the new self, which is being renewed in knowledge in the image of its Creator. Here there is no Greek or Jew, circumcised or uncircumcised, barbarian, Scythian, slave or free, but Christ is all, and is in all. (Colossians 3:9–11)

Just as Christ transcends all barriers and unifies all people from all cultures, so God's man makes no distinctions.

Shakespeare's contention that "all the world's a stage, and all the men and women merely players" is biblically consistent. History is a captured thought, a story, an acting out of an epic adventure—and we all must play a part. And at the end, there's a curtain call. The key, according to the Bible, is to be aware of this dynamic and actively take part in it. Within *His*tory is our story.

"For we are God's workmanship, created in Christ Jesus to do good works, which God prepared in advance for us to do" (Ephesians 2:10). It's weird to think about my story being God's artistic expression, but that's exactly what it is for God's man. Our lives are God's workmanship and the choices we make are a part of the play he is writing. What's inconceivable to me is that I get to take part in the final scene by the choices I make now.

Be aware: opposing forces are at work to get you to serve yourself. But Jesus said, "Not so with you." Secure the victory for someone else, just as Jesus secured the victory for you.

chapter 5

taking the hit

It's not what we take up, it's what we give up that makes us rich.

—HENRY WARD BEECHER

"Kenny, it's Bill."

"Hey, Bill. What's going on?"

"Listen, Kenny. Do you have a minute? I need to ask you a question about something."

Pause. "Absolutely. Fire away," I said.

That was a lie. A truthful response would have been, "No, I don't have a minute or another second. I just finished a board meeting, I'm under titanic pressure to finish this project, and I'm getting frustrated with all the interruptions!" That was my reality. But I wasn't going to make Bill suffer for what he didn't know. I love the guy. So I lied. (Is that wrong?)

After placing my mental schedule on the altar, Bill shared with me what was giving him a spiritual fever. "I led a group of junior high boys last year for church," he explained. "All five are signed up again this year, and they want me to be their leader. The church promised I would have a co-leader to help out, but I just found out it's still just me. Should I say yes anyway? Brian [his eighth-grade son] really wants me to lead it, but I want to make sure I'm doing it with the right motives and not out of obligation. I have so much going on with work right now."

While Bill told me his concern, I thought about a conversation I had just finished—with God. Sixty seconds earlier, I had prayed about a little kafuffle of my own, saying, *Lord, would you help me find a good story about what it means to sacrifice?* I had written down the word *sacrifice*. Next to it, I wrote, *to suffer loss; to give up; or to renounce for an ideal, a belief, or an end.* Ever notice how God has a sense of humor? Bill couldn't see me, but I was shaking my head, a big smile on my face as he presented his dilemma.

"Bill, I am as maxed out as I've ever been. I need some margin in my life." I could relate to Bill, but I also thought of how all men must, in the words of Andrew Jackson, "pay the price to secure the blessing." It was the blessing piece that I didn't want Bill to miss,

> *Ever notice how God has a sense of humor?*

which meant I had to tell him what his faith—and not his feelings— needed to hear. It was clear he was looking for some affirmation to do what he knew he needed to do—sacrifice his own comfort for the sake of his son and those boys. And I was truly impressed with Bill and his relationship with his son. When I was in eighth grade, choosing to let my dad leak all over my friends on a weekly basis would have been second only to being caught in a public place in my underwear. But for Bill, this was a true gift and he needed to know how rare an opportunity like this was. I didn't hold back.

"First of all, that's amazing that eighth-grade boys want to charge the hill with you—again! That says a lot about you. More important, think about five years from now when Brian is graduating from high school and leaving to go start life as an adult. Picture yourself sitting in the stands with Carol bawling, and you're looking down at Brian walking in his cap and gown. Look back at this moment and ask yourself if it was worth what you gave up to lead him and his friends that year back in eighth grade."

Bill was quiet for a few seconds and then I heard him inhale. "I never regret it. In fact, afterward, I feel great. Thanks. I needed to hear that."

He kept talking, talking himself into it. I just listened, observing Bill's thirst for significance overtake his fear. He had to determine what was worthwhile before committing himself to sacrifice for it. And once he did, he didn't need me. Duty deconstructed the dilemma for God's man. Soon there was no dilemma at all. The negatives were all gone. Sacrifice morphed into a positive duty, creating a positive perspective. He had worked it through in his mind, considered his feelings, and now reluctance was gone. His reasoning: a decision for himself would have died with him. Instead, the sacrifice he made for his son would remain.

Bill was leaking Jesus—he took the hit for heaven's sake. He intentionally gave up time to rest after work for something better. He felt odd but good about his decision. Why? It is what he gave up that makes him rich and helps him live out God's dream for his life. He held on to God's dream by letting go of his own dreams. He found Christ by losing. It's counterintuitive, but it makes all the sense in the world through his eyes of faith. His likeness is morphing. He ceases to be Bill by becoming somebody new—God's man.

The son, by the way, will hear just one thing: "I'll be there for you." Bill's son may never know what his dad went through to be there, and he shouldn't. Only Bill knows, and that's why it's called sacrifice—it's a personal giving up known only to the one making it. No one else should fully understand it at the time. It is made without immediate reward, benefit, or notice. We receive the reward of our sacrifices in the future.

Personal sacrifices are the grinding wheel of sharpening character. A grinding wheel makes sparks fly when the blade is sharpened. The wheel causes friction, but the friction is what gets the results. Or look at it this way:

> The pig and the chicken were on their way to breakfast trying to decide what to have. The chicken said, "Let's have some ham and eggs." The pig replied, "That's fine for you; it's a small donation on your part, but it's a total sacrifice for me."

For me, the pig was too nice—he's gonna take the bigger hit. With proper levels of testosterone, Porky would have said, "You want some ham? I'll give you some ham!" Then he'd have proceeded to take Mr. Chicken behind Old McDonald's shed and squeeze the E-I-E-I-O out of him. The audacity of the chicken's suggestion suggests he wasn't thinking of who he

dream fact
Donation without sacrifice is not significant.

was with and was responding simply with his own comfort in mind. But brother swine was not codependent with his poultry pal. He makes it clear that a donation without sacrifice is not significant. In fact, it's plain old self-preservation.

When we take any action of significance, the realization of personal cost is the challenge. Accepting the cost means sacrifice. Bill's version of the story ends with the pig becoming a willing pig.

Later Joy

Men hate to defer pleasure. Wait for something? Oh, man, sign me up! (Cough, hack.)

We are creatures of the moment because we are creatures of the flesh. And the flesh knows only one space-time continuum—*here, now.* Yet if I have a certainty of a future payout, a promise that the cavalry is coming, a definite delivery date of the dream, I can endure a great deal. For God's dream to be realized in your life, the training is more about endurance than quickness. We are called to endure a great deal and sacrifice experiences, moments, and seasons for a payout that may not come in this life. Why? Because endurance through sacrifice was Jesus's character and expression.

To want Christ means to want to become a man who can sacrifice whatever and whenever. And when we make our peace with that, God's dream for us makes progress. Any attempt to blend the dreams of earth with the dream of God in Christ will force you into losing yardage for the kingdom, and you'll be struggling to kick field goals instead of scoring touchdowns. Trying to do both doesn't lead to the Super Bowl of significance.

The good news is that God does not ask us to sacrifice for sacrifice's sake (masochism). He "incentivizes" us. Jesus laid out the incentive structure: "But seek first his kingdom and his righteousness, and all these things will be given to you as well" (Matthew 6:33). To do that involves acts of self-limitation on a continuous basis.

As God's man G. K. Chesterton was working through this whole idea of sacrifice, he came to a radical conclusion in his book *Orthodoxy:* "Every act of will is an act of self-limitation. To desire action is to desire limitation. In that sense every act is an act of self sacrifice. When you choose anything you reject everything else." And when we self-limit for the sake of God's plans, the strong and simple promise (according to Jesus) is that our sacrifices will be honored by God in His time, His way. That's how Jesus lived His life and how He wants us to live ours.

The "not as I will, but as you will" life is a life of self-limitation for a cause and for a payoff. The question is: are you willing to sacrifice in order to secure the blessing of becoming like Christ?

A defining characteristic for every God's man seeking greatness is this: he sacrifices to secure a blessing. Not to sacrifice is to forfeit the reward. He is either in a condition of gaining or losing rewards based on what he is giving up. The strong encouragement, example, and experience of Christ is deeply connected to our own willingness to live a life of continuous sacrifice—a life driven by the solid expectation that our sacrifices for Him on earth will be richly rewarded.

Sacrifice and glory held a symbiotic power for the Son of God. They were two separate and unique experiences that were mysteriously working together for present greatness. This same connection between present sacrifice and future glory is meant to be equally in you as you seek greatness in God's power.

"Therefore, since we are surrounded by such a huge crowd of witnesses to the life of faith, let us strip off every weight that slows us down, especially the sin that so easily trips us up. And let us run with endurance the race God has set before us. We do this by keeping our eyes on Jesus, the champion who initiates and perfects our faith. *Because of the joy awaiting him, he endured the cross, disregarding its shame.* Now he is seated in the place of honor beside God's throne. Think of all the hostility he endured from sinful people; then you won't become weary and give up" (Hebrews 12:1–3, NLT).

> **dream fact**
> *If we are willing to sacrifice now for God, we will experience the joy of our reward later.*

Every one of these you give up for your relationship with God is an opportunity to bring Him glory:

- an attitude
- a behavior
- a response
- a comfort
- a right to strike back
- a feeling
- an impulse
- a chance to control
- a grab for power
- a portion of your time

- a pattern of your old life
- a financial bonus
- a freedom
- a way of doing something
- a golden opportunity

There are a lot of great concepts in the passage above describing Jesus's heroic sacrifice on the cross. But the three words that make a life statement about Him in the area of sacrifice are "He was willing." From start to finish He was making sacrifices. From leaving heaven for earth right through to how He would leave earth for heaven—it was all one big sacrifice followed by a ginormous celebration and coronation: "Now he is seated in the place of honor beside God's throne" in heaven. He is in the place where glory resides through His sacrifices.

> *The road to glory is paved with sacrifice.*

The road to glory is paved with sacrifice.

Acts of the Will

We woke up at 3:00 a.m. Our flight left at 6:00 a.m., so it was "wheels up" from our hotel at 3:30 to get to the airport, return the car, catch the shuttle, check in, and get to our gate. Our ministry team had just concluded a two-day conference in North Carolina. The effect of the conference was tremendous: many decisions for Christ, many dramatic recommitments to the Lord, as well as twenty-five new men's Bible studies planted in the community. Flying home after a conference like this is always torture. It's like coming in from war, following a massive firefight for forty-eight hours and trying to reserve any remaining energy after battle. Your battlefield acuity is still way up, but your mind and body are shut down. I carry more fatigue on the way home than I do luggage.

The simple goal: find a bunker and sleep.

The first leg, I sorta, kinda, half succeeded. I got a few winks, but they only left me more dazed and confused. My head felt like a sack of cement on drugs—dead weight but full of racing thoughts and disconnected concerns. When we connected at Dallas, my seat was in an exit row—I was stoked. Leg room!

You know the drill: board by group number, moo-moo down the cattle shoot to your seat. Silently (and very selfishly), I prayed that the person sitting between me and the guy with the goatee in 19A had had an accident. Any sort would do. Just so that it would prevent his taking up space in my row. To my infinite delight, the person in 19B never came. *Yes!*

I eyeballed the guy in 19A, buried in papers and work. *Good. I'll just read the conference evaluations until I can sleep, and maybe I won't be a total crusty grump for Chrissy and the kids when I land in three hours.*

I looked quite busy, my pen out, making notes, shuffling paper, responding to an associate in the opposite row. Thirty minutes in, I sensed exhaustion winning. Total shutdown imminent. Happily, I stowed my evaluations, reclined the chair, and started to put my headphones on when I noticed a face to my left leaning toward me.

Incoming!

"I thought I was the only one working hard on a weekend," he said.

Oh no. A conversation starter! I am so depleted. I can't talk to anyone anymore. "Yeah, well, I have a writing deadline on top of my other stuff," I said. I shoot a glance at the manual he was reading earlier and notice he works in the same field as a friend of mine—geotechnology. What are the chances of that? So I quiz him on the usual info, searching for connections. He found out that I really do understand his work and we began talking engineering. I was reaching for a good segue, and the only one I could think of is to the Master Designer who loves this guy and wants to know him. So I decided to share with him the engineering story I use to help explain faith.

A nap? Huh-uh. Nap is bye-bye.

Turned out my engineering friend, Mike, was going through a family crisis and was seeking solutions for helping out a family member.

"When the engineering is shaky on the inside," I told him, "the infrastructure wobbles. And when it's under pressure it collapses, resulting in various forms of damage and destruction. So what you need to do is check the engineering of the character which will explain the conduct, and work it backward. See? You go after the character to reengineer the conduct."

I sat back. *Oooooh. Aaaaah. That was good.* I was happy with myself.

But God wasn't.

Suddenly the Holy Spirit impressed on me to keep going. I pressed on, giving a quick version of my testimony, and asked him directly if he'd ever made a decision like that.

I jumped off the cliff and waited…

Mike told me that he and his fellow university professors regularly discussed religion and philosophy, and there was one question that eluded explanation: what's the main difference between Christianity and the rest of the world's major religions? To him they all felt the same. Fair enough.

I was not eager to evangelize to the man in 19C.

Fifteen minutes later I was led to ask not just a question but *the* question: "So, Mike, have you ever done something like that—prayed a prayer of introduction to Jesus Christ to start that relationship?"

"No."

"So what's stopping you?"

"Based on what you just told me—nothing."

I smiled. "Then take my hand, bow your head, and repeat my words to invite Christ into your life."

"Let's do it."

After we prayed, we exchanged numbers to plan a future meet up. I invited him to my next conference, and he said he would come. I told him I'd send him a Bible and that a friend of mine from a church in his area would give him a call about a men's group he could plug into. He was all smiles and very grateful.

He was also low-hanging fruit.

As we got off the plane, a couple behind me said, "You were busy!" They said they'd been praying for my conversation with this guy, and they rejoiced when I told them how he'd committed his life to Christ. As we walked to the baggage claim, I just kept saying, "Wow." I was not in a good place. I was not "in the mood." I wanted to disengage, unplug, and isolate. I was not excited about the opportunity. I was not eager to evangelize the man in 19C.

But in the end, I was willing.

"Wow" expressed my state of disbelief. The fact that God knew my condition and called me to stretch, trust, obey, and sacrifice my moment of comfort proved to me that the tapestry of salvation is woven with the thread of sacrifice. A few minutes, a few words, a few stories. "Wow" reflected the very nonsupernatural appearance of a very supernatural moment when we least expect it. "Wow" expressed my healthy fear when I realized what would have happened if I'd turned inward when turning outward was necessary. "Wow" conveyed my joy in having made the right choice. And "wow" described the look on my family members' faces as we all sat on my daughter Cara's bed while I told the story that night.

From exhaustion to salvation. Wow.

And finally, afterward, I slept. The perfect end to a perfect day.

> You can't live a perfect day without doing something for someone
> else who will never be able to repay you.
> —John Wooden

Future Glory

Jesus was rich with sacrifice. He sacrificed His time, energy, and efforts. He sacrificed the comforts of home to connect with people. He sacrificed recognition of men for reconciliation of men to God. He sacrificed energy to take care of others, trusting that God would replenish Him at the proper time. He sacrificed His right to get even with His killers. He sacrificed earthly recognition, comfort, approval, pleasures, power, and possessions. He did so knowing that His sacrifices were not unnoticed. More, He knew that beyond recognition would be celebration. He knew He was scoring touchdowns for God on earth versus sitting out, losing yardage, or settling for field goals. He was even hungry enough to go all the way and lay down the costliest sacrifice of all upon the altar of others' free will, and didn't try to force anyone into heaven.

Every sacrifice for God is a touchdown. Big or small. His dream for you is to make a man who is willing to do what

> **dream fact**
> *The ultimate example lives in you.*

is required for the kingdom—in a marriage, at work, in a trauma, in the third world, or in seat 19C. Conversely, the character of Christ cannot form in the heart of a man who is not willing to sacrifice the things of earth for the glory of heaven. The key to real sacrifice is believing that the glory of God is more important than anything you're giving up.

The ultimate example lives in you and dreams of the day He will share this same glory with you.

> As for me, my life has already been poured out an offering to God. The time of my death is near. I have fought the good fight, I have

finished the race, and I have remained faithful. And now the prize awaits me—the crown of righteousness, which the Lord, the righteous Judge, will give me on the day of his return. And the prize is not just for me but for all who eagerly look forward to his appearing. (2 Timothy 4:6–8, NLT)

Make the sacrifice today.

chapter 6

fully qualified

Dare, dare, my dear brethren in Christ, to follow the Captain
of your salvation, who was made perfect through sufferings.

—GEORGE WHITFIELD

John Sidney McCain III is a very public man. He is the son and grand-
son of two U.S. Navy admirals. Both were heroes, one in Okinawa and
the other in Vietnam. He's an accomplished naval aviator who narrowly
escaped death numerous times and cemented a reputation as a risk taker.

He has big, bizarre tales of survival. Once he was forced to eject from a
crippled aircraft after an accidental rocket shot from the deck of a carrier
and hit his plane as he was taking off. He jumped into the flames as
bombs from his own plane ignited and exploded.

Can you imagine the adrenaline?

Here is a man who possesses hero status. A war veteran and decorated
military servant, his honors include the Silver Star, the Bronze Star, the

Legion of Merit, the Purple Heart, and a Distinguished Flying Cross. He's a living G.I. Joe—a man of mythical exploits. His background has led to a stellar political career as U.S. senator for Arizona since 1986 and recent presidential candidate.

However, these accomplishments are not why the world respects him so deeply. America has many decorated veterans and solid politicians. Even heroes. But John McCain is set apart by his experience as a prisoner of war and the suffering he endured over five and a half years at the famous Hanoi Hilton in North Vietnam.

> *He jumped into the flames as bombs from his own plane ignited and exploded.*

The details were widely reported:

- On October 26, 1967, McCain's A-4 Skyhawk was shot down over Truc Bach Lake. He broke both arms and legs after ejecting from his plane.
- He was found by the enemy, mobbed, and stripped naked.
- He was then tortured by North Vietnamese captors who crushed his shoulder with a rifle butt and bayoneted his groin and feet before bringing him to Hao Lo Prison, also known infamously by American POWs as the Hanoi Hilton.
- He was interrogated daily and was beaten unconscious when he refused to provide any information to his captors.
- He refused an offer of repatriation, a special exemption for the son of a commanding naval officer, and elected to extend his stay at the "Hilton."

- Under torture, he signed a propaganda statement which was later deemed unusable by the enemy. When they tried to get McCain to sign a usable statement, he flatly refused and suffered three beatings a week for it.
- He was released from captivity in 1973.
- To this day, John McCain cannot raise his arms above his shoulders due to multiple fractures from the beatings.[2]

From these details, we can see why John McCain's experience transcends him and simple comparisons of pain and anguish. He would probably be the first to point out that he is one among many who suffered and that he was fortunate to survive captivity when so many lost their lives. No, the true influence, the true power of the man lies in the coalescing of his experience, personality, position of leadership, and circumstances. While skepticism clouds most leaders' reputations, there is a respect, reverence, and high opinion of this man across the political spectrum.

The separating factor for John McCain is the reality that few men possess the personal experience that impacts his choices in political office. He is respected differently, listened to differently, and is able to achieve what few people in Washington can claim: *a suspension of any skepticism about his loyalty.* People may question or disagree with his views, but no one can question his sincerity. Why? Because when it comes to the topics of leadership, liberty, freedom, international relations, and courage, his layover at the Hanoi Hilton qualified him to speak more accurately and passionately than most anyone.

McCain's suffering gives him an authentic appeal and character. The spin of savvy talk show hosts cannot compete with a leader who has suffered greatly for his loyalties and remained steadfast. It's not just about being a senator; there are many of those. A war veteran can be good senator— three other U.S. senators are also Vietnam vets. But a good senator who suffered greatly for his country is worthy of unique honor. Great senators, in the presence of John McCain, do not peacock. They are bound by the old adage that "he who walks tallest drinks first." Retired Captain John McCain walks tall as a leader.

When a man suffers nobly, he earns the kind of respect that knowledge and service alone cannot touch.

The Turning Hour

It might happen on the commute home from work. *Wham!* A guy side-swipes you on the freeway and your car tips and starts flipping. Three kinds of suffering begin to unfold: for the driver of the car who hit you, for you, and for the witness.

1. *Consequential suffering.* The guy who hit you gets jail time for driving under the influence. This will diminish his character and pollute his ability to lead.
2. *Accidental suffering.* You did not see him coming, and you suffered multiple fractures. This garners sympathy, and the process of physical therapy and rehabilitation garners admiration and inspires.
3. *Noble suffering.* A driver passing saw the accident, noticed the flames, and stopped to pull you out, suffering second- and third-degree burns. His suffering stands apart from the first two, catapulting his status because of the cost he paid. He made an honorable choice and suffered for it. This is a turning hour that has great impact on this man's life.

You get the point: there is an inflictor, the inflicted, and then sacrificial suffering. This last kind is rare and exceptional. Only one makes a man great.

It can also make a generation great.

George Washington had his share of suffering during the American Revolution. But he most admired the men who served under him, knowing they experienced far greater physical and emotional hardships than he did. In the winter of 1777–78, Washington was low on supplies, and his men were paying the price. Starving, freezing, and exhausted, they worked in deep snow to build log cabins for the winter. Washington was in awe of their willingness to put up with so much for the cause of liberty.

In one of his letters asking for supplies and relief for his men, Washington wrote, "A part of the Army has been a week without any kind of flesh, and the rest three or four days. Naked and starving as they are, we cannot enough admire the incomparable patience and fidelity of the soldiery, that they have not been ere this excited by their suffering to a general mutiny or dispersion."

These guys blew Washington's mind. Why? Suffering showed their true character, which turned out to be shockingly noble. Washington reasoned that their suffering should have brought mutiny. Men should wilt under those conditions. But this was different. The pain they endured for the cause of liberty put one of history's greatest men in a state of amazement

> **dream fact**
> *Suffering shows*
> *our true character.*

and respect, likely coupled with a stark realization of his unworthiness and powerlessness (that's the definition of awe, by the way). That's the feeling you get when you are around men who are suffering nobly in their turning hour.

The turning hour of a man's life is when he nobly accepts suffering for something greater than himself. This noble willingness makes men out of boys. It is responsible and mature. It is driven by a belief that some greater context encapsulates the suffering and gives it meaning. The cause becomes more significant than his suffering. So he endures it willingly, patiently, and aggressively.

By contrast, an unwillingness to suffer catastrophically stops a man's growth and precipitates regression. Good men don't have to suffer to keep their status in the world's eyes. "Don't rock the boat." "Just provide for your family and secure a good legacy." But for God's man, moving from good to great means embracing a turning hour in your spiritual journey where belief in Christ grows into a willingness to pay the price for that relationship and its purposes in your life. In its most basic sense, comfort and Christlikeness do not blend.

This is the final frontier for God's man. Personal discomfort naturally follows the quest for Christlikeness. It is uncommon ground to the natural or carnal man—those that use worldly reasoning as the basis for their decisions. Coasting or giving up on the goal of maturity must be replaced by diving aggressively into greatness through ever-greater sacrifice. This embracing of the full cost is rare, the exception and the challenge. Most men with good intentions have mutinied and dispersed rather than endured to discover God's full dream. That's because good intentions are no substitute for great faith in a man's character. There are no substitutes for the willingness to trust, come what may.

My son, Ryan, is learning this at an early age. In the highly competitive world of club soccer, this proud papa has seen that he has a great athlete for a son. Of course, so do all the other dads on this elite team of "futbolers." Every year Ryan must try out to make this special squad, and he has done

> ### dream fact
> *Comfort and Christlikeness do not blend.*

so for three consecutive years. As they have risen through the ranks of Southern California teams, the best players on other teams have tried to displace my son from his spot. To remake the team, he committed to training four days a week for six months. He made it, but for the first time he is not starting and not playing the whole game.

This is a huge blow. For a twelve-year-old, this is suffering. It is a constant battle not to get discouraged, especially on game days. I know he hates this season of discontent. I know he wonders why. He must be asking himself, *Why did I train so hard for this?* He has never faced this sort of test before. For my man, this is a turning hour—a time when he could choose to mutiny inside, get critical and cave. Or he could show what he is made of, trust God's control over his life, and keep training hard.

It's painful to watch this as a dad, but I see in this opportunity how everything depends on whether Ryan goes with his feelings and quick-fixes or whether he turns to God and his dad for help. If he can turn to God, this turning hour could be one of the greatest of his young life. If he successfully weathers this season of roller-coaster emotions, disappointment and disillusionment, it will firmly plant an invisible heavenly Father behind a visible time of suffering.

So we are trusting God together, and I am asking my heavenly Father to make this the beginning of a great man who does not worry when suffering comes. I am asking Him to teach him, to grow him into what he wasn't before. I know what I don't want to happen. I don't want him to respond like many men I counsel do. They believe suffering is a curse from which to flee versus being a sacred trial allowed by God to make him like Christ. These men miss their hour by turning and heading for the hills either emotionally or physically. And in doing so, they prove themselves boys. I know you have seen it in yourself and in other men, because we all have caved at some point. Yet the result is always the same: they become harder toward God, smaller as men, and poorer for their pain instead of richer.

"The Christian faith has not been tried," writes Phillips Brooks. "Not until men get rid of the thought that it is a poor machine, an expedient for saving them from suffering and pain, not until they get the grand idea of it as the great power of God present in and through the lives of men, not until then does Christianity enter upon its true trial and become ready to show what it can do."

In other words, a relationship with Christ is ultimately not a pacifier but a passion producer that leads God's man to do the unnatural, the unsafe. When suffering comes, God's men seek God's purpose in it. That choice makes God's man great, qualifies his faith, and makes him most eligible to be a leader in God's kingdom.

The comfort God's man gives up allows him to take up more of Christ. To these ends, God's man, you must assess your own experience with God's power and your connection to it: how much have you been willing to endure, bear, and undergo for Jesus in your times of pain? Ask yourself, *Am I a finisher or a safety seeker?*

Opportunities to give up the comfort zone for the cause of Christ come up in every man's life. Individually, relationally, or emotionally, these divine moments must be seized in uncommon ways—ways that will not soothe or reassure your feelings and fears. These day-by-day choices will call

> *The comfort God's man gives up allows him to take up more of Christ.*

your faith out on the carpet, expose it, and define it for years to come.

Sanctified Pain

Every form of pain endured for Christ is holy because you're aligned with Christ who suffered pain in every form. Christlikeness requires believing that God has authority over suffering. It is a mind-set that knows suffering achieves His dream of molding you into the image of Jesus. The Son suffered, and the adopted sons must be perfected like Him through the same sorrows, griefs, disappointments, and pains of earth. The Father refined Jesus into greatness and glory as our leader, and now it's His dream for you. Through your sufferings (chosen and circumstantial), you will grow into God's man.

Without God's authority over suffering, the idea of holy pain is ridiculous. Without God's authority, God's man becomes stoppable in his suffering. Life dishes out its worst, and it can crush you. But if your suffering is preempted with a deep and abiding trust in God's sovereign control of all things, you will prevail. "The reason my Father loves me is that I lay down my life—only to take it up again. No one takes it from me, but I lay it down of my own accord. I have authority to lay it down and authority to take it up again" (John 10:17–18). The Man who said these confident and courageous words lives in you.

Christ's suffering was never master over Him. And in a stunning blow to evil, Jesus proclaimed mastery over His suffering by choosing it out of

> *Christ's suffering was never master over Him.*

love for the Father and acceptance of His cause. This was His turning hour as the Son of Man, choosing suffering as the path to greatness. This is His greatest imprint and highest example for followers seeking to be great.

And possibly even more unbelievable, you and I were the reason for this entire thing! "God, for whom and through whom everything was made, chose to bring many children into glory. And it was only right that he should make Jesus, through his suffering, a perfect leader, fit to bring them into their salvation. So now Jesus and the ones he makes holy have the same Father. That is why Jesus is not ashamed to call *them* his brothers and sisters" (Hebrews 2:10–11, NLT).

"Them" is us! Jesus Christ made us His brothers by making pain holy in three specific ways. These transformational truths on suffering have serious implications for God's man.

1. *Suffering made Christ fit to lead.* Funny that it wasn't theology, training, or miracles that qualified Jesus to lead you and me. None of these would make Him the perfect leader. Only His willingness to give up comfort for us and His Father made Him ultimately worthy

of being our Captain. What does this tell us about real leadership? It is not an intellectual pursuit or strategy—it is not a formula. True leadership for God's man means we give up personal comfort for a cause and have a willingness to go all the way.

2. *Suffering is what connected us to God.* Through the suffering of Jesus, the active power of the Holy Spirit agented your salvation and connected you to God. If that is what initially united you to the Father, what do you think most powerfully joins you to Him today? The same active power inside of the sufferings of Christ is also pregnant inside of your present and coming afflictions. God is ready to release power through your suffering to make you more like Christ and bring glory to Him. Suffering makes possible both a powerful relationship and experience with God if we let Him have it. If we keep it for ourselves, seek to avoid it, or solve our suffering with Christless solutions, we will miss the power of this ultimate fellowship of God.

3. *Suffering for God's purposes unites us with Jesus.* The power of a shared experience cements relationships. Just ask a group of war veterans who saw action together. Surviving mutual suffering is an experience that goes beyond any suffering endured in isolation. What made these war vets into bands of brothers is what makes Jesus unashamed to call us His brother. The shared experience of suffering for our Father's kingdom binds us inextricably to the Person of greatest power. "No man," wrote Thomas à Kempis, "hath so cordial a feeling of the Passion of Christ, as he that hath suffered the like himself."

Want to feel more united to Jesus right now, brother? Do the hard thing, the thing that will make you wince. Do it for God. Do it wherever the holy discomfort lies. You will feel the brotherhood in a more profound way than yesterday. This is the yell of the heart for every true God's man:

I didn't want some petty, inferior brand of righteousness that comes from keeping a list of rules when I could get the robust kind that comes from trusting Christ—God's righteousness. I gave up all that inferior stuff so I could know Christ personally, experience his resurrection power, be a partner in his suffering, and go all the way with him to death itself. (Philippians 3:9–10, MSG)

Suffering pierces through the mystery of God and unites you to Him. More important, it qualifies you to lead in His kingdom work.

No man wants to suffer. But God's man does not fear it because it unites him to his King. That is why we must lay down our own comforts, safeties, predictabilities, sureties, insecurities, fears, and prideful stances. Then we must pick up our crosses to experience God's ultimate vision for us. The what, where, when, why, and how is locked inside God's mind alone, and it will come to life as you willingly subject yourself to His way, in His time. To endure this kind of suffering will look like a tragedy to the outsider. But to you it will be the fruit of your undivided allegiance.

Trust in God and His purposes in the pain. God's man, don't let suffering disturb you. If you're suffering, it has been allowed by God in your life. Let it come. And know that it comes with great purpose in your life—to bring the greatest nobility possible—to become like our Brother, Jesus.

No leader in God's family has a greater connection to the cause of the kingdom than the man who has suffered to give it control in his own heart, relationships, and world.

What do you say to that? Yes.

chapter 7

my Father's will

God's will is not an itinerary but an attitude.

—ANDREW DHUSE

Our Dad can be a real stickler about how we use our time.

My own dad was huge on time. Sometime in the late sixties my dad received a genuine navy ships clock. It was mounted to a glossy mahogany back-plate in the shape of a small shield. No big thing. The clock itself was another story—it was nautical art.

Imagine sailing the open sea in a Yankee clipper ship, full sails open, wind in your face. You are the helmsman. You take in the horizon with deep satisfaction as your hand rests ever-so-commandingly on the big wooden wheel at your fingertips, the helm that controls the rudder and, consequently, the entire ship. Its handles are made of the finest wood, seaworthy and hearty. The wheel rotates fluidly, smoothly, and efficiently as you bring the great ship about and carve the horizon in search of glory.

Now picture that helm in high polished brass, shrink it down to twelve inches in diameter, and you have the setting into which the face of the clock sits like a diamond solitaire. The round window covering set into the wheel of the helm resembles a port hole on a ship. It's made of thick clear glass with a half-inch rim of brass encircling its circumference, acting as both a window and shield for what lay underneath—time itself.

Two circles of cannonball-black numbers shout out the time—civilian time, the larger set, each number underscored by a smaller, perfectly aligned, military counterpart. The hands of the clock are so precise, the tips of the elongated spades click off one hundred and twenty half-minute hashed lines on a graphed strip edging the clock's face.

When you stand before it, taking in this clock, you notice two evenly spaced holes located just above and on either side of the number six. These are the winding holes. A small hook attached to the bottom of the mahogany mount holds a heavy, stainless steel key. Once a week the face

> *The clock itself was another story—it was nautical art.*

of the clock is carefully removed and the key is alternately inserted into the winding holes and given a particular number of turns—eight being the appropriate number. The clock wound and the port hole closed, the clock is returned to its place above the mantle in the living room.

This clock may look like art, but it acts more like a cannon every thirty minutes when the bells toll. You hear the spring mechanism click in sync with the exact second the long hand reaches the six or twelve, and then, after a millisecond pause, time is told. An even number of chiming bells is given on the hour. Odd number on the half hour. Eight various bells are struck on four-hour cycles, giving the corresponding time stamp for night or day.

And yet the clock is "time by sense and feel" more than by sight and sound. My father treasured this clock. It spoke volumes about his priority of punctuality. I would ask permission to leave the house and my dad would say, "I want you back by eight bells."

"Okay, Dad," I'd say, knowing that I would return to the door at precisely 11:55, or all hell would break loose. My dad could hear those bells in his sleep, from down the hall in his room in the back of the house. At night, if his conscience decided it was time to check on Kenny, he would get up at eight bells and check to see if I was standing there.

Time was a sacred consideration to my dad.

Growing up under this filter of time-is-life and life-is-time, I became very sensitive about time. Specifically, I saw my dad's navy sense of punctuality as a purpose lived out every day. I'd hear him at one bell in the morning (4:30 a.m.) getting his lunch together for work and fixing that one-egg sandwich. He'd often make comments after hearing the bells about orders of business in the house: "Time to shower." "Time for the news." "Time to go to bed, Ken." When my mom was gone or unable to take me to things, I loathed those bells for reminding him of the pending trip because it meant arriving up to two hours early for whatever it was.

My dad was never late. And consequently, neither was I.

Driving Forces

I must have seemed an odd little shaver because I was always hours early to Little League games, school, church, practice, whatever. Like father, like son. Funny thing is, my dad never once mentioned the importance of time to me. Yet through his modeling, I assimilated it seamlessly into the fabric of my life. His attitude toward time was adopted and integrated perfectly. I saw it was important to him and, subconsciously, I became equally sensitive to time. In fact, I still am—just ask my wife. I was in a hurry once and left her in the church parking lot by mistake. I had the kids; the ship was leaving port. I got on the freeway and after five minutes, the realization.

Thanks, Dad. The bells tolled for me that day!

Fathers project priorities and those priorities reflect their will. In this sense fathers become, almost by default, the driving forces of our lives. One friend told me that when his wife notices his dad's character coming out of him she calls him by his dad's name. It's not a positive experience for him, but he can't seem to help himself. The list of my father's will would look like this:

- respect (assumed by position)
- discipline
- hard work
- accountability
- authority
- self-sufficiency
- control (his)
- command (his)

- compliance
- punctuality

I saw my dad's will in each area. I felt it in the home. I adopted it as a priority. This alignment with his will was always good for him, sometimes good for me, and sometimes good for others.

You might be thinking, *Hey, wait a minute, Kenny. The list I see looks awesome.* I agree; my dad's will does look very industrious and manly. The punctuality thing, for example, was morally benign, easily absorbed, and mostly good. However, alignment of my will to my dad's wasn't driven by relationship. It was precipitated by his role and rule over my life. If I rewind the tape, what's clear to me is that my connection to my father's will was either based on approval and acceptance or based on pain and fear. Because I knew his priorities, I would submit to them, knowing he would affirm me in those—affirmation I rarely experienced but desperately wanted.

I knew, for example, that if I mowed all three lawns, cleaned out the garage, and kept my room spic and span, he would notice and likely respond with an, "Atta boy." This was to me what a crack hit is to a junkie. I also knew that if I got out of line, disobeyed an instruction, or delayed my response to anything I knew was a priority, he would take notice and respond negatively. Instead of a crack hit, I'd get cracked.

> *My dad's praise was to me what a crack hit is to a junkie.*

Dad's nickname was Godzilla. Godzilla doesn't reason or talk anything out—he crushes it. Dad's will and my will had an emotional-behavioral dynamic versus a character-relational one. I adopted his will to garner his affection or avoid his anger, not because I'd experienced the importance or value of his will. One mode of adopting the father's will is reaction based; the other is relationally based. One is based on fragile emotions; the other is based; on agreement with his will based on knowledge of his character.

One is healthy; the other is not.

Any man who reacts to God's will out of a crushing fear of losing His favor or stirring His anger inevitably ends up resigning, resenting, or resisting His will. Fear and mixed motives always mess up a good thing.

The Main Thing

Christlikeness is all about the Father's will.

In your journey to realize God's dream for your life, God's will must be at the forefront of your mind. What is God's will? It's directly reflected in the character of Christ. In Jesus, we see an aggressive freedom to pursue, articulate, and accept His Father's will. In his connection to the Father's will, God's man sees it, feels it, adopts it, integrates it, and is individually motivated to pursue it.

God's dream for you is identical.

In the Gospels, Jesus presents a powerful picture of His Father as the creative mind and Himself the primary agent for its expression on earth. It is a dynamic relationship rooted in love, intimate knowledge, and a mutual commitment to accomplish very specific purposes. Before Jesus had healed one person, cast out one demon, or preached one message on the kingdom, an emphatic Father laid the foundation for His Son's fulfillment of His will by cementing their bond. It's a bond we will experience when we begin to venture successfully into the Father's will.

Rooted in Unconditional Acceptance

> When all the people were being baptized, Jesus was baptized too. And as he was praying, heaven was opened and the Holy Spirit descended on him in bodily form like a dove. And a voice came from heaven: "You are my Son, whom I love; with you I am well pleased." (Luke 3:21–22)

The relationship was solidly intact because of the expression and unique awareness of the Father's acceptance and affirmation of the Son, independent of his exploits.

Jesus hadn't done a thing at this point and *boom!* a nuclear-sized expression of love on the part of the Father toward His Son. All fear is dispelled, rebuked, and restricted from winning over the heart of the Son because it's full of a Father's love. With this type of love pulsating from His Father toward him, Jesus could afford to emotionally and relationally live for an audience of One and the will of One. He would not need the approval or acceptance of men. This made Him fearless in His focus and pursuit of the Father's priorities for His time on earth.

Rooted in Intimate Knowledge

> I tell you the truth, the Son can do nothing by himself; he can do only what he sees his Father doing, because whatever the Father

does the Son also does. For the Father loves the Son and shows him all he does. (John 5:19–20)

This is a picture of mutual cooperation, the sharing of intimate knowledge, modeling, relationship, and love. There is a dependence on knowledge Jesus possessed of the Father that guided His own expression of His will on earth. He did not need to check it out with religious leaders of his day, modern thinkers, or the Roman authorities. He owned the Father's heart Himself. God's will had been plainly revealed and, therefore, would be plainly and authoritatively expressed in His life. Jesus's knowledge of the Father's heart kept His actions focused and pure in spite of His surroundings.

Rooted in Mutual Cooperation

Jesus said to them, "My Father is always at his work to this very day, and I, too, am working." (John 5:17)

The free exchange of feeling and thought between Jesus and God was a synergy of purpose the world had never seen. It was the Father & Son Redemption Co.: "Building the kingdom since 33 A.D." Because the Father loved the Son so deeply, He revealed His plans and purposes to Him, and the Son obediently carried them out. Over and over we see Jesus reference Their mutual commitment to executing a specific blueprint. He would say things like:

- "My food is to do the will of him who sent me" (John 4:34).
- "I do nothing on my own but speak just what the Father has taught me" (John 8:28).
- "These words you hear are not my own; they belong to the Father who sent me" (John 14:24).

- "For I have come down from heaven not to do my will but to do the will of him who sent me" (John 6:38).

Multiple statements like these reveal Jesus's unwavering commitment to God's purposes in the world. Jesus did not adopt His Father's will for selfish purposes, to garner His affection, avoid His anger, or experience a reward. For Jesus, it was a direct outcome of personally experiencing, seeing, and assigning importance to God's purposes as a willing agent of expression. We see a Jesus who is functionally attached to the Father's will and free to make it His mission. Loved, accepted, secure, knowledgeable, ready, sent, and focused, we see the God-Man equipped to take His Father's heart to the fullest extent possible.

So what about you? What is the connection to you? According to Jesus, the exact same dynamics apply, custom designed to produce the same high octane and spiritually healthy commitment. Observe Jesus's prayer for you:

- "I in them and you in me. May they be brought to complete unity to let the world know that you sent me and have loved them even as you have loved me" (John 17:23).

  Translation: "Father, root them in your love by helping them see, accept, and embrace Your unconditional acceptance, the same acceptance you have for me. Then cut 'em loose!"
- "That they may know you, the only true God, and Jesus Christ, whom you have sent" (John 17:3).

  Translation: "Give them an intimate, close-up knowledge of You through Me just like I have an intimate close-up knowledge of You. Help them model Your character, share Your heart and plans, and duplicate what they see in Our relationship."

- "As you sent me into the world, I have sent them into the world" (John 17:18).

    Translation: "They are going to work with us and commit to finishing what we started."

He did His Father's will. We watched. We start to do it together. We do and He watches. And then, finally, we do it! We do our Father's will as willing sons: thoughtfully, intuitively, and aggressively.

Like Jesus.

Jesus Bros. Inc.

Every family tows the line with a certain code of behavior. Among the men in my family, this includes certain types of pinches, jokes, heckling, one-upping, kissing (Guamanian tradition), conspiring over practical jokes, body noises, and ministering wherever and whenever possible. Oh, and eating—gross, ungodly amounts of eating. What a combination! You sense danger on the edge of this delight, knowing you've entered a new world not for the weak-hearted. This is what it feels like around Luck men.

You will get sucked in if you're within five-hundred yards. We just don't care. These behaviors represent our bond, our benchmark for inclusion in the inner circle. Anything less suggests an acquaintance. Our family is a fraternity complete with hazing, rituals, ceremonies, and tests of brother-hood. We are positively chemical at times.

The idea that fraternity and cultures of behaviors are inherently bad was probably foreign to Jesus. There is a consistency of culture in fraternities of men that speak to their integrity of identity. Jesus played upon that to highlight the gaps in integrity as he taught men what it meant to belong. In fact, He would play sergeant at arms about the acceptable conduct of His so-called followers. He would recall followers and have closed-chapter meetings for the express purpose of exposing and weeding out those guys who were posing. He would not comfort them—nor would He confront them maliciously. He would simply challenge their identity as God's men by correlating their behaviors with His express will.

He would say things like, "Why do you call me, 'Lord, Lord,' and do not do what I say?" (Luke 6:46). The identity of God's man, according to Jesus, leads directly to a responsibility to His express will and integration into your life. He never qualified statements like this; He would lead with them! Jesus was particularly loath of

> **dream fact**
> *"Whoever does the will of my Father in heaven is my brother."*

the groups of men who posed as superspiritual on the outside but were betrayed by their motives. These guys were dysfunctional, unattached to God's will. To these men, he would quote the prophet Isaiah and double sting them: "Isaiah was right when he prophesied about you hypocrites; as it is written: 'These people honor me with their lips, but their hearts are far from me'" (Mark 7:6). The blade of truth cut both ways; both internal beliefs and external behaviors were examined for authenticity of commitment and consistency with the Father's will.

Membership in this brotherhood boiled down to one thing: "For whoever does the will of my Father in heaven is my brother" (Matthew 12:50). This involves a spectrum of actions and attitudes that are easily recognized by other believers under the Great Commandment.

You know when someone's main conviction is loving God and loving people. Like Jesus, they are free in the fight. They don't need to see all the variables in most decisions, only these two important ones. That eliminates doubt and distraction in their spiritual affairs. It is not complicated. In fact, when a man starts to complicate God's will repeatedly and regularly, there's reason to question.

God's dream for you is to be a doer of the Father's will. That's as opposed to being a:

- discusser of His will
- debater of His will
- deconstructor of His will
- dissector of His will
- deflector of His will
- delayer of His will
- dealmaker of His will
- doubter of His will

This life of doing the Father's will is a combination of promise and persecution, blessing and suffering. Our fraternity accepts both the joys and tribulations of being Jesus's brothers. The best news is that Jesus Christ accepts all men into His brotherhood and all men can begin today to do the one thing that distinguishes a brother of Christ: the will of the Father.

What does that mean for you? How far are you willing to go? For God's man, the Father's will is made easier by the Father's love. We see that commitment to us and we find ourselves more committed. We see His sacrifice of His Son, and we find ourselves more willing to give up comforts of our own. For some of us, we do not doubt that the Father's will is best as much as we wonder how uncomfortable the "best" will end up being. Trusting God in your personal Garden of Gethsemane will be what bonds you most deeply to His image.

Martin Luther may have spelled out what it means to do the Father's will better than most when he observed, "I have held many things in my hands, and I have lost them all; but whatever I have placed in God's hands, that I still possess." In the end, that is the essence of doing the Father's will—placing yourself in God's hands right now. Then you will be like your Brother, Jesus.

> My Father, if it is possible, may this cup be taken from me. Yet not as I will, but as you will. (Matthew 26:39)

This aspect of Dad's dream is simple: Want more of His will and less of yours. Today and tomorrow. In big and small.

Make Dad your dominant influence.

chapter 8

locking eyes

Sons are for fathers the twice-told tale.

—Victoria Secunda

Did your dad ever give you "the look"? Ryan and I lock eyes all the time.
And I'd love to report that my face's color and expressions are always in-
fused with love. But they're not. I can report, however, a good many of
them are, and that my son knows his dad is present, watching, and waiting to encourage him.

If you asked him, he'd tell you about all the nonverbal ways we commu-
nicate. Sometimes the connection is just with the eyes and a nod of my
head that says, "I love you." No words. Sometimes our eyes will lock
when he's taking the soccer field and I'll hand signal *I love you* in our
unofficial father-son sign language. Again, not a word. Still other times a
touch is the vehicle.

From the time he was a little shaver, three intermittent squeezes of a hand
or leg or arm communicated how we felt—one squeeze for each word.

Squeeze–*I*–squeeze–*love*–squeeze–*you*. His response back would be the same, and then he would hold up two fingers. *I love you too*. This continues to the bedside routine. At the end of our prayer, the *amen* is three rapid kisses on the cheek, followed by three cheek-sniffs (Guamanian tradition again). Another one is the infamous surprise backrubs (the kid has the best hands in the family). Again, talking without saying a word. Suddenly I'll just feel these strong hands massaging handfuls of my shoulders. I respond positively (usually by unbridled groans) and eventually he slaps me on the back three times and disappears without a word.

Ryan loves me. To say we have a deep connection is inadequate. But that's our bit.

With my dad, you didn't want the look. If you got the look, the hand or the belt was sure to follow. To this day, I can't believe how powerful the facial expressions of my father were to me. His face determined the whole atmosphere of our family and, sadly, there were not many, if any, smiles on my pop's face while I was growing up. The colors of his face were (1) pale when he was sober, calm, and rested, and (2) red all the other times. I used to try to read his face to get a sense of his mood and determine what might happen next and, many times, to avoid what might happen next.

Fortunately, the end of the story with my dad is bright. At sixty-five, he began a new spiritual journey and finished strong in his relationships. I never saw his face turn red after that. Even though I was married with three kids, I was so glad to be my dad's son during this time. The reciprocity between us was rich, from his spiritual renewal, to his heart bypass, to when we finally buried him to the sound of taps, and I bawled like a baby.

There is a profound sense of joy that penetrates the soul of a father as he locks eyes with his son. With a father and his daughter, it's more of a protective instinct, as a commission to guard a rare and priceless diamond. With a father and son, it's a more potent generational instinct, passing on the legacy and seeing yourself in him. I can't explain the feeling—wanting to be noble, to translate and transmit that sense of honor into Ryan's life.

It haunts me to think of those invisible demons of character that have the potential to limit me from being the type of man

I can't believe how powerful the facial expressions of my father were to me.

I desperately want Ryan to see and become. But when we lock eyes, I find renewed power to fight those demons, to prevail for him. This bond reflects the bond between Father, Son, and the Holy Spirit: the creative source of the Father, the agent of expression in the Son, and the invisible power of the Holy Spirit that makes it all happen.

In those moments, I feel eternity. No words. A satisfied smile tells it all.

Ryan can fear me, rebel against me, hate me, love me, resent me, miss me, or want me as his father, but the overriding message I see from him is this: he really wants me to see him being a good person and doing good things he knows please me. It's very personal and special to me and him exclusively. It's not something we talk about. It's like we share this connection and both of us are pulling for each other—him for me and me for him. It's not about performing a task or achieving a mission. It's about making the other person happy.

We want to see each other win in the big arenas of our lives. It's not about duty; it's about the bond between us. It's not about his fulfilling a mission. It's about delighting a dad and cheering on a son. It's not about some final accounting that will happen in the future. It's about us drawing closer as father and son. There is no gun to his head. Ryan wants to, in the purest sense of the expression, make my day.

We see this kind of relationship between Jesus and His Father—this kindred fellowship of Son and Dad—reciprocity, an intuitive-relational bonding of spirit.

Family Ties

There are two separate aspects to Jesus's relationship with His Father. In chapter 7 we talked about the first aspect: Jesus's awareness of the Father's will and His laserlike focus on the objectives He was sent to secure. He's all business. It's the Father's purpose He must fulfill, the Father's words He must share, and the Father's work He must finish. We see Jesus acting out of His true identity, His duty to that identity, and the job responsibilities of that identity as the God-Man. He is a tasked man, partnering with "him who sent me." And God recognizes and rewards His son with position, ruling presence, and power. The focus is on the work His Father gave Him and the stewardship of His time on earth.

The Father & Son Redemption Co. was making it happen for the kingdom:

> Then a cloud appeared and enveloped them, and a voice came from the cloud: "This is my Son, whom I love. Listen to him!" Suddenly, when they looked around, they no longer saw anyone with them except Jesus. (Mark 9:7–8)

Here we see Dad emphatically supporting the Son and the Son emphatically partnering with Dad. The focus was on execution of the mission—a mission Jesus reported directly to His Father upon completion:

> I have brought you glory on earth by completing the work you gave
> me to do. And now, Father, glorify me in your presence with the
> glory I had with you before the world began. (John 17:4–5)

A divine initiative had been consummated and was now to be celebrated. His kingdom came and His will was done. This is a picture of the public Jesus with the assigning Father—a working relationship.

Yet Jesus's private knowledge of the Father is much more "dad-centric." In this part of Jesus's life, He's not acting out of duty, identity, and responsibility to the Father's will. He gives us a more personal sense of His motivation—one that acts out of love for His Abba Father. There's an awareness that Dad's watching His life and relating to Him as a Dad.

Equally, the Son is pursuing a way of being that delights the Dad. There's not a lot of demonstrative communication—it's more about simply being, which is a powerful witness of the Spirit. Like me and Ryan, it's not about public messaging; it's about the Father and the Son locking eyes. It's about masculine intimacy.

In the Know

Jesus Christ loved His exclusive relationship with the Father and the fact that no one knew Him better. He prided Himself on the limited access to their personal relationship. The ground was sacred. They shared a deep and satisfying connection unique just to them. What made it special was the inside knowledge of the other. No human being would ever know Jesus as intimately as the Father and vice versa. This dynamic was not and never will be divulged, diminished, or distilled for anyone. However, God's man is ushered by Christ into this same exclusive relationship with the Father to possess and treasure a unique bond with the Father just as He did. "All things have been committed to me by my Father. No one knows the Son except the Father, and no one knows the Father except the Son and those to whom the Son chooses to reveal him" (Matthew 11:27).

That's you, God's man. Have you realized your intimate relationship to the Father?

"Know" Substitutes

Jesus Christ did reveal some aspects of how His Father and Son relationship worked with His Dad. He drew the analogy to the familiarity and relationship a shepherd has with his sheep. The sheep knew the voice, body language, whistle, and call of their shepherd. We see the dynamic of the exclusivity of their connection to him. Just as the sheep share a unique awareness and knowledge of their shepherd, Jesus possesses that kind of rare connection with the Father.

Surrogate shepherds didn't work because the familiarity and comfort the sheep had with their true leader, provider, and protector was polluted by a strange voice. Astonishingly, the Good Shepherd laid down His life for His sheep to give you a chance for an intimate connection. "I am the good shepherd; I know my sheep and my sheep know me—just as the Father

> **dream fact**
> *No one knows you better than the Father.*

knows me and I know the Father—and I lay down my life for the sheep"
(John 10:14–15).

No one knows you better than the Father, just as no one knew Jesus
better than His Father.

You Know Him Too?

The idea of sharing your dad with a newly adopted sibling can be a difficult adjustment for some children. There's a fear that the special love for
the natural children will somehow be diminished. But the vast majority
of children freely and willingly share their daddy with their newly
adopted family member. You could have been an adoptive threat to the
relationship between Jesus and the Father. But thank God, Jesus didn't
feel that way. In fact, His desire is for you to experience the exact fullness
of relationship with the Father that the original and only Son possesses.
"Righteous Father, though the world does not know you, I know you,
and they know that you have sent me. I have made you known to them,
and will continue to make you known in order that the love you have for
me may be in them and that I myself may be in them" (John 17:25–26).

The only Son wants you to experience and enjoy sonship with His
Father. Have you fully embraced your adopting Father as Dad?

Symbiotic Sonship

Christlikeness is all about sonship with the Father. God's dream for you
is to experience, as Jesus modeled, true fellowship and reciprocity with
Him. Take a second and absorb that. Let it sink into your soul: your
heavenly Father is seeking you out, His beloved son.

Because those who are led by the Spirit of God are sons of God. For you did not receive a spirit that makes you a slave again to fear, but you received the Spirit of sonship. And by him we cry, "Abba, Father." The Spirit himself testifies with our spirit that we are God's children. (Romans 8:14–16)

God wants that special connection with you right now. He wants to lock eyes. He wants a one in a billion connection with His son. He wants you to feel that profound sense of honor He feels that makes Him want to transmit His nobility into your life right now. He's dreaming of all you can become.

All fathers have dreams for what their sons could become. But in this case, there's an important difference. This Father can't disappoint. There are no haunting thoughts or demons of character that can sabotage His deepest wishes and visions for your life. Nothing can ever prevent Him from being the prime example of what He wants you to become. His dream is to be the creative force in your life, for you to be an agent of His expression, and to give you the active power to pull this off through the Holy Spirit.

He wants you to experience eternity as a firstborn son.

This offer is lost on many men of faith. They don't get it, don't see it, don't experience God's anointing and adoption upon their lives as His sons. In other words, they miss the dream. Instead, out of ignorance or plain stubbornness, they reject the extended hand of their loving Father. And His longing for sonship with them goes painfully unfulfilled. Only a true dad's heart could say, "How gladly would I treat you like sons and give you a desirable land, the most beautiful inheritance of any nation. I thought you would call me 'Father' and not turn away from following me" (Jeremiah 3:19).

Wait a minute. Did God think wrong here? Or was it that His protective, empowering love was so strong, He simply could not accept the rejection? Bursting with emotion for us, the wound makes no sense to Him. Maybe this is beyond what we can understand, but maybe it was that the thought of rejection was impossible, even for God.

Think of the prodigal son story and His bottomless love grows even clearer. He knew others might reject him, but his own boys? What would I do if the sons I'd die for dismissed me and trashed my strong fatherly affection? I can't imagine.

How about you? Are you practicing the sort of sonship that makes you feel like a firstborn son? Are you seeking a special revelation from your Father, since we're told He already has all revelation concerning you? Are you hearing His call to you daily? Do you know His body language, His smell, His special whistle?

Or is there something in the way?

Today you can begin to lock eyes with your Father. Right now, you can start living out God's dream for you of sonship. Jesus tells us clearly how it should feel and how it should look when there is Father-to-son missile lock.

Listen to the voice of experience.

Sonship Is Authentic

Yet a time is coming and has now come when the true worshipers will worship the Father in spirit and truth, for they are the kind of worshipers the Father seeks. (John 4:23)

Above all, the Father loves sons who are real with Him. When we come, we come with all that we are without apology or pretense. It's His joy to see you—scabs and all. We practice transparency with Him the way all innocent children let their daddies into their world. We engage Him as He is—our Father who sees us—the good and not-so-good in us. That's when we connect.

So, God's man, are you artificial or authentic with your heavenly Father?

Sonship Consists of Private Interaction

But when you pray, go into your room, close the door and pray to your Father, who is unseen. Then your Father, who sees what is done in secret, will reward you. (Matthew 6:6)

I will never forget the night I told God that I wanted to see Him. Can you believe the audacity? I was seventeen and searching, no manipulative or selfish motives. I went into my room, closed my door, and in the most truthful way I knew, I told God, "I want to see You." No one was in the room with me until my Father who sees came. That night, for the first time I felt a Father's love, and I have never stopped seeking that behind closed doors.

dream fact
God delights in a private audience with His son.

Some things should never change, like having private conversations with your Father and sharing private things with Him first before friends, spiritual partners, spouses, or colleagues. He is always waiting, and He delights in a private audience with His son.

Where would you like to see your Father show up in your life right now? Have you asked? How's the dialogue going? He told me to tell you this, "I'll be there."

Sonship Is Attention Enough

> But when you give to the needy, do not let your left hand know
> what your right hand is doing, so that your giving may be in secret.
> Then your Father, who sees what is done in secret, will reward you.
> (Matthew 6:3–4)

In our culture of approval addiction, crises of character can result when people place too high a value on the opinions of men. We can easily fall into a sort of schizophrenic routine of alternately loving and loathing the opinions of others around us. Thank God for sons who care less about man and more about what the Father thinks. Sonship causes the lines men use to separate themselves from each other to blur or even disappear. The Father should be the only audience that matters.

A son who seeks the Father's attention gets the Father's attention. The reward is His awareness, His presence, and His affirmation. It's made of the stuff true fathers and sons feel and share together. Is your heavenly Father's approval enough? Or are you seeking other validation?

Live As a Son

Becoming like Christ means learning how to live as a son, how to trust your Father so intuitively and implicitly that conscious communication gives way to an internalized, symbiotic sonship. You can go from guessing to knowing what He is feeling and respond to that as your guiding force. You can know His desires as His son, know the look in His eyes, the nod of His head.

Yes, you can be this close. In God's dream, you belong to Him. Consider this belonging to be the distinction between vocational worship and relational sonship. One flow is time and people driven. The other flow is presence and Father driven. One is a public process of mutual partnership and investment in a co-mission. The other is a masculine dance of soul and knowledge between Father and follower. According to the Scriptures, both of these dynamic relationships are meaning oriented, but only one is personal, extending into the realm of a family tie that binds closer than all others.

Jesus Christ was tight with his Dad and they loved to make each other smile. That's sonship. This is our prime example of this uncommon connection of reciprocity between two souls.

So, Son, get to know "the look." And walk like your Dad.

chapter 9

aspirin with skin

Compassion alone stands apart from the continuous traffic of
good and evil proceeding within us.

—ERIC HOFFER

On December 8, 1941, my mother heard the sounds of war for the first
time in her life. Imperial Japanese air squadrons were sinking a frigate,
and strafing and bombing the Marine installation.

Shock and fear coursed through her. Only days before, talk on the island
had been about how the Japanese would never take on the United States
in a head-to-head battle for the island. The wishful bubble burst that
morning. For the Chamorros on the island, panic, fear, and chaos set in.

On December 9, the island was surrounded by the Japanese invasion
force, and in the early morning hours of December 10, five thousand
Japanese began landing on numerous beaches, all headed toward the
capital of Agana (a-GAN-yuh). The island was surrendered the same

day as the Japanese commander-in-chief issued an ominous proclamation and posted it all over the island. My mother read these words:

> We proclaim herewith that our Japanese Army has occupied this island of Guam by the order of the Great Emperor of Japan. It is for the purpose of restoring liberty and rescuing the Whole Asiatic people and creating the permanent peace in Asia. Thus our intention is to establish a New Order in the World.
>
> You all good citizens need not worry anything under the regulations of our Japanese authorities and my [sic] enjoy your daily life as we guarantee your lives and never distress nor plunder your property. In case, however, when we demand you [sic] accommodations necessary for our quarters and lodgings, you shall meet promptly with our requirements. In that case our Army shall not fail to pay you in our own currency.
>
> Those who conduct any defiance and who act spy [sic] against our enterprises, shall court-martialed and the Army shall take strict cause to execute such criminals by shooting!
>
> Dated this 10th day of December 2601 in Japanese calendar or by this 10th day of December 1941.
>
> By Order of the Japanese Commander-in-Chief.[3]

The altruism was a lie, but the threat of reprisal was not. My mom was a part of this page in human history of suffering and survival. My mother recalled many memories with laserlike accuracy:

- hiding radioman First Class, USN, George Tweed for the duration of the occupation, the only American soldier not killed or captured by the Japanese

- a dogfight and eventual crash of a Japanese Zero by an American P-38
- hiding an American flag in her bra and praying numerous times every day for the Marines to come
- the concentration camps on the southern part of the island and the abuse of women at the hands of the soldiers
- the massacres, including decapitations of loved ones
- the compassion of a Japanese officer my mother's family knew as their angel

"Angel"

Her first recollection of him was that he spoke perfect English. According to my mother, he was a Japanese national who had been sent to the United States to receive his college training at Harvard shortly before the war broke out. He returned home and was quickly drafted, trained, and commissioned as a naval officer, assigned to the Asiatic Expeditionary Forces. Once the Japanese had stationed troops throughout the island, sent captured Americans to prisons in Japan, put a curfew in place, and seized all communications, army rule gave way to naval rule of the island in the spring of 1942.

"Angel" was part of this new rule.

For two and a half years, my mom was a prisoner of war in her own home. The horror of the invasion gave way to resignation, passive coop-eration with authorities, and a constant fear of rape and execution. My mother's family was singled out and tracked down by the Japanese com-mand because my grandfather, Baltazzar Carbulido, was an educator on the island. Japanese respect for *sensei* (teachers), combined with their initiative to train teaching assistants, landed my grandfather in favor.

My mother, along with several of her girlfriends, was to be trained as a translator. This training interrupted their forced labor in the rice fields. It was during this time their angel first appeared, in full officer's regalia, sword on his hip, riding high upon an imperial navy-issued horse. His presence was directive-only—no personal involvements. But as the tide of war shifted toward the Japanese, his heart began to leak out in behaviors that would have led to immediate court-martial and execution.

According to my mother, the period of relative calm ended abruptly with the bombing of the Orote (Or-ROW-tee) airstrip. The face of occupation turned evil once again. The Japanese drafted every available male into labor battalions to build everything from air-raid shelters to pillboxes to gun emplacements. Apathy prevailed as Guamanian men and women labored under the worst of conditions, kicked, punched, and clubbed by their Japanese supervisors. Concentration camps were set up in several locations to prevent local islanders from assisting the American liberators. The islanders began to experience the worst massacres yet—Guamanians forced into caves, entrances sealed, and grenades thrown in. Men shot and thrown into trenches they had just dug. Hundreds of men carrying food and ammo to Japanese positions were gunned down and decapitated.

> *My mom's "angel" would have faced immediate court-martial and execution.*

Yet during this darkest time, the angel was busy.

- He warned my mother's family of the coming American Marine invasion and the expected retaliation that would put the family in danger.
- He rode to where my mother's family was hiding in the jungle to give instructions on where to hide from Japanese patrols that were capturing men and women for forced labor. Three times his information saved them.
- When they were finally caught, he followed my mother's family through their captivity and made sure they were assigned work in the rice fields.
- He protected my mother and her girlfriends from becoming "comfort women" for Japanese commanders.
- He warned them of potential massacres and provided escape plans. My mother remembers watching the feet of Japanese soldiers passing by her concealed holes in the jungle floor, praying for them to have blind eyes.

Recently, I called my mom's younger sister Helen (now in her seventies) to confirm the stories and gather more details. She confirmed all of them and offered something more I wasn't quite prepared for—deep gratitude for this man, over sixty years later. In a very delicate and barely audible voice, she said, "We called him our angel. I wish I knew his real name. He needs to be recognized." Her voice cracked and choked on the other end. One man's compassion was still alive and speaking to me. And we didn't even know his name!

My own existence very likely hinged on this one man's compassion in the midst of that awful time during World War II. I doubt I'll ever be able to thank him or his family. I don't know what motivated him to put his own life in jeopardy like that, and I never will. But I do know that of all the great war heroes from every age, none will ever take the place of this compassionate warrior known only to me as our angel.

> You can accomplish by kindness what you cannot by force.
> —Publilius Syrus

Ask the Leper

Compassion gladdens the hearts of those who travel the road of pain.

My mother felt so helped in the midst of her battle for survival. In her prewar comfort, the acts of kindness on the part of that Japanese officer would never have had the effect of emotional tsunamis in her soul like they did in the midst of war.

The message: *You have not been abandoned.*

My mom's story is dramatic. But you don't need a world war to create a context for compassion's power. Every day that Jesus walked the earth there were plenty of battles being fought—physical, emotional, political, relational, and psychological—into which His compassion found a place. Without compassion, Jesus could not have met the demands of the realities He came to address. And as His agent and ambassador, neither can you. His example did not presume compassion alone could eliminate evil entirely, but He could mitigate it, engage and resist it while on earth.

> *Compassion gladdens the hearts of those who travel the road of pain.*

That's what made Jesus, Jesus. It's what makes God's man, God's man.

And in the process of seeing that need and responding in the character of Christ, God's man can send a message more powerful than any deed and tower over lesser accomplishments. Compassion becomes its own law, delivering with overpowering strength a higher authority, a signature of God.

Jesus's messages of overpowering compassion were loud and clear.

The Message of Identity

A man with leprosy came to him and begged him on his knees, "If you are willing, you can make me clean." Filled with compassion, Jesus reached out his hand and touched the man. (Mark 1:40–41)

The freedom to touch the untouchable came from an identity free of the opinions of man, free of the compulsions of culture, and free of the pressure of politics. Compassion lets the world know you are free to be God's man. You act for an audience of One. This is a rare thing. It is attractive. It is Christlike. He saw the man, His heart responded, and His identity in the Father released Him to reach out, not cop out to the politics of clean or unclean. God's dream for you is that you would be equally strong and secure in Him so that the compassion of Christ could flow freely to those who need your touch. Compassion established Jesus as a God pleaser versus a man pleaser. Our freedom to touch and meet needs is always a reflection of our identity.

The question is, how free are you to touch the untouchables?

The Message of Reality

When Jesus landed and saw a large crowd, he had compassion on them and healed their sick. (Matthew 14:14)

Numerous places in the Gospels reveal Jesus's process of acquiring a visual (He saw), reacting internally (compassion), and then responding (healing, touching, feeding, teaching, or exhorting). The compassionate responses of Christ are not possible without willingness to visually and emotionally connect with reality. In stark contrast to the spiritual leaders of His time, His visual awareness of need caused Him to respond with compassion, versus allowing His rational mind to excuse Him.

Compassion is the simple difference between denying reality and embracing it. "He saw" is the headline of compassion in the life of Christ—eyes wide open. Wherever He went, He was willing to do what He could in the moment. Jesus would see people without food, empathize with their plight, and make provision to feed them. He would see grieving people, experience an internal reaction, and weep with them. He would see directionless people, react with compassion, and start teaching them. By Jesus's very life we see that compassion means being responsible with the fragile realities around you. "Not my problem" was not in Jesus's vocabulary, because the people around him were a part of His reality.

Compassion comes from seeing reality and not running from, denying, or hiding from it. Not self-absorbed, Jesus was free to see reality and act. Some He could fix in the moment. Others would take a while. And still others would have to wait for His return. But that did not stop Him from acting.

If you are afraid of truth and reality, you will have a distant expression of compassion. Ask yourself, *Do I embrace reality and work with it, or do I rationalize running from it?* You will see a direct connection in your ability to act compassionately.

The Message of Dignity

> But a Samaritan, as he traveled, came where the man was; and when he saw him, he took pity on him. He went to him and bandaged his wounds, pouring on oil and wine. Then he put the man on his own donkey, took him to an inn and took care of him. (Luke 10:33–34)

It is more important, more than anything, to recognize who the Samaritan is here. This Eagle Scout is a hated foreigner, but Jesus dignifies him with hero status. Jesus gives us a triple scoop of dignity here drowned in compassion. Again, notice the progression: "he saw" and then "he took pity." He transfers over from his own life what was lost by the man who was robbed, beaten, and left for dead:

- He replaces his own position on the donkey with that of the hurt man.
- He replaces his own agenda with the mission of helping the man.
- He replaces the man's inability to pay with his own payment.
- He gives up his time to minister to the man.
- He gives away his own dignity in order to restore the dignity of another.

The actions speak louder and clearer than any possible words. The Samaritan truly jumped inside the hurting man's skin and didn't allow himself to be at peace until he'd restored peace for him. That is the best working definition of compassion one can find and the best picture of restoring dignity—by divesting yourself of your own.

Sound familiar? The ability to demonstrate Christlike compassion is intimately tethered to our own willingness to be undignified. The question to ask yourself is: *How undignified am I willing to be in order to meet the needs of another?*

The Message of Urgency

> When he saw the crowds, he had compassion on them, because they were harassed and helpless, like sheep without a shepherd. Then he said to his disciples, "The harvest is plentiful but the workers are few. Ask the Lord of the harvest, therefore, to send out workers into his harvest field." (Matthew 9:36–38)

The Greek word for compassion here is *splagnizosthé* (which sounds a lot like what it means): "from the gut." Jesus wasn't punched, but He was dealt a blow to His gut. And, based on what He saw, He reacted as we have now come to expect—His heart broke because of the distress of others. He dwelt on (versus dismissing) what He saw long enough to make a correlation in His own mind that stiffened His resolve to act. Except this time He couldn't meet all the needs by Himself, so He projected His gut onto those around Him with, shall we say, energy.

> **dream fact**
> *Compassion always leads to urgency.*

The message: there is no such thing as a compassionate delayed response! If Jesus couldn't alleviate the suffering Himself, then He'd enjoin God, prayer, His disciples, and every other means necessary to help Him. His compassion was a catalyst creating a sense of urgency in those around him. His purpose: get their eyes open to share in the responsibility.

It would be easier to accept defeat. The problem was too overwhelming for one man. Don't lay a guilt trip on anybody. But no. Not the God-

Man. He would not allow himself to miss this opportunity. Waiting would have made it too late. Compassion always leads to urgency. Ask yourself, *Does apathy or urgency define my response to others' pain?*

The Message of Accountability

> Then the King will say to those on his right, "Come, you who are blessed by my Father; take your inheritance, the kingdom prepared for you since the creation of the world. For I was hungry and you gave me something to eat, I was thirsty and you gave me something to drink, I was a stranger and you invited me in, I needed clothes and you clothed me, I was sick and you looked after me, I was in prison and you came to visit me." (Matthew 25:34–36)

Man may dismiss compassion in the moment, but God never, ever does. It does not matter where you sit theologically concerning *when* the words above will be spoken. They *will* be spoken. They will be spoken to men who might believe at that moment that they have pulled the wool over God's eyes. That somehow God passed over this compassion requirement. But He measures our commitment on this moral value of compassion. Intellectually knowing someone is not enough. You need to understand what is important to a person and adopt their concern as your very own.

Eternity and the people who share it with their King will share one quality: compassion for those in need and the character to act on it. In fact, history for each of us will culminate in a cosmic act of compassion on God's part. "He will wipe every tear from their eyes. There will be no more death or mourning or crying or pain" (Revelation 21:4). God's compassion triumphs in heaven, alleviating our losses, suffering, and pain. The main reason we cannot shake off the needs of others is because God never shakes ours off! He keeps meeting them until our peace becomes

His peace and we can both rest. Compassion, in the mind of Jesus, is the sign and sealer of salvation, making us accountable to the very end.

Holiness is compassion and compassion is the highest form of holiness. Ask yourself, *How do I define holiness? Do I allow myself to see, feel and act like Jesus, or do I dismiss need?*

When the Bible says, "Your attitude should be the same as that of Christ Jesus," you can't miss His character of compassion (Philippians 2:5). If His dream for us is Christ Himself, then God looks at you and sees that there is nothing so basic to your identity as compassion.

> Every man who eats should remember those who starve. And each man who rejoices in the Gospel should have compassion on those who never heard it once. Jesus did!
> —Stuart Briscoe

Tenderness Is Fearlessness

Apathy is to indifference as tenderness is to compassion.

When you look at Christ the King, you see the tendency toward tenderness. It is upside-down in man's world but right-side-up in God's world. A true measure of courage is willingness to be tender when compassion demands it. Inability to be tender is fear—of man, of appearances, or of reality, which hides an even deeper fear of responsibility.

Ouch! I'm killing myself here. Intimacy with people is not my strong suit. But I know it's reachable because, "I can do everything through him who gives me strength" (Philippians 4:13). And He says that His character, which includes recognizing pain and acting with compassion, can be formed in me.

What would show the world that a man's heart is free to respond to the Holy Spirit? Answer: tenderness. To his tenderness he must add timeliness, and to his timeliness he must add toughness, for the time to act does not respect circumstance. God's man, like his King, only concerns himself with meeting the need.

Start in your immediate circle of influence and ask yourself, *Will I wimp out or step into those needs with compassion? Will I offer a gentle touch or rationalize it away? Will I let myself see the pain instead of trying to fix the problem? Will I give away my own dignity to restore someone else's?*

These are some of the bigger questions I am wrestling with myself. Maybe you, like me, have not graduated from the school of compassion. I actually trained myself not to feel. To survive as young man, I fought the feelings battle. It's become a life habit. But I am relearning how to be tender, to be fearless in Christ. And I'm discovering that this compassion and tenderness costs me very little. Yet it accomplishes so much in the lives of others when I simply have the courage to act on it in faith. This keeps my willingness to risk high.

But I still struggle to apply it in my day-to-day life.

That's why John Hall hits me like a shot to the jaw when he says, "Kind words, kind looks, kind acts, and warm handshakes. These are the secondary means of grace when men in trouble are fighting their unseen battles." *Smack!*

Compassion is not about me but about fighting for others. Now *that* I connect with. I love helping people fight their unseen battles in the name of Jesus. But to do that, I have to develop discernment and sensitivity to see when the battle is raging. I need those eyes to see. I learn the most by studying Jesus, getting a feel for His rhythm, and recognizing that emotionally tough situations are the exact moments when He's calling me to care.

Slowly I am coming to a new definition of manhood, one rooted in tenderness as a sign of spiritual toughness. I am beginning to feel the truth that the best parts of my life will be the forgotten acts of compassion that were remembered by God. I am learning that compassion trumps condemnation every time and that practical empathy provides needed emotional shade to the sun-baked and weary soul—a comfort, a relief, a pause that allows that person to forget their pain and find hope again.

Jesus's tendency toward tenderness and comforting others in pain is well documented. His kindness never weakened His stamina or softened His fiber—it just made Him stand out more as a leader. We see Him move about freely in extending compassion, but we don't see someone who met every single need. What we do see is a man moved by need who allows the need to move Him. His tenderness made Him both feared and fearless.

> **dream fact**
> *"Apathy is the glove into which evil slips its hand."*
> *—Bodie Thoene,*
> **Munich Signature**

In this sense, the dream is simple: be moved and move.

chapter 10

seeing past

The outward man is the swinging door, the inner man is the
still hinge.

—MEISTER ECKHART

Men are like icebergs—you only see the tip.

Take Jim. He came up and met me on the stage after I'd spoken at a
men's conference. He shook my hand and said nothing. His face looked
drained, yet happy at the same time. He would not let go of my hand.

Shaking his head slowly, he remained silent. Tears streamed down his
cheeks.

After about ten full seconds of this, I decided to just relax. I looked into
his eyes and let his death grip do the talking for him. I wasn't going to
rush him. After another ten seconds, which felt like an eternity when
holding hands with a crying guy in front of lots of other guys, he finally

opened his mouth. A big deep breath came out and, like a pressure lock, he simultaneously released my white hand, and it returned to its natural shape and color.

"Thank you," he said, stepping back from me a little, locking my gaze. "Thank you so much."

Then, like a ghost, he disappeared.

A few weeks later I noticed a handwritten envelope in my inbox. It was sticking out of a pile of letters I needed to go through, so of course, I grabbed this one first. The ones penned by a hand rather than a printer look like scrolls of ancient Rome these days. Very rare. Instantly, I know these special notes are either from a correctional facility or overseas. I was right—sort of.

It was from a man who had just been released from prison and could not have a computer under the terms of his parole. It was the ghost man from the retreat. He was reappearing now to answer the question he couldn't over that weekend. He needed to share

"Daddy, there are some policemen here to see you."

what was going on below the waterline of his iceberg. Every word I read revealed the titanic reality I could not see before, what he could not reveal previously. Here it is:

Dear Kenny,
I came back to church after my arrest in 2003. Married for 20 years, 4 kids, a great house, a career as a journalist, active in the community, and a faithful servant at church. And then, at age 40, I risked it

all for a relationship with a teenage girl I met on the Internet. I risked it all and lost. My victim's mother found out. Two days later my five-year-old came to tell me, "Daddy, there are some policemen here to see you." I was on the front page of my local newspaper.

Slapped back to my senses, stunned by the depths of my fall, I grasped at anything I could. I immediately committed to a weekly men's group. The men I met in that group heard and knew the worst about me—and yet loved me. When I went to prison, they kept in touch, visited me, and, I know, prayed for me.

I got out of prison two years later. My wife divorced me three days later. I am not allowed to see my children. So this conference was the reunion of sorts that I had looked forward to for three years—three LONG years—and I was not let down. Six of us from the original group roomed together. I was blessed beyond belief and, when I encountered you that night, beyond words. I wanted you to know why. You know the story of the four men who carried their sick friend and lowered him through the roof to see Jesus? I am on the stretcher. That man is me. So, as I said the other night—thank you.

Jim

Seventy-five percent of the men who attend my conferences are fighting to slay the dragon of sexual compromise. Of the married guys, over 50 percent are having major marital difficulties. Over 90 percent are managing a stress-producing crisis or personal problem that they want help with. The rest are faking it.

You may not be guilty of Jim's vice, but that's because you have a different one. His sin is the kind society loves to reprove. The sins of other men are more "respectable," so naturally, many would love to step up to throw stones. Yet if Jesus said to us, "If any one of you is without sin, let him be the first to throw a stone," the thud of rocks dropping from our hands would come quickly (John 8:7).

In fact, Jesus did say that to us. His vision always penetrates below the waterline. One of the surprising dynamics of the Every Man conference is that the Holy Spirit often uses it to drop sea level on men's icebergs. Almost imperceptibly, the authenticity in the room creates transparency, transparency creates vulnerability, and that vulnerability creates a weird sort of masculine intimacy (which is an oxymoron, of course). The emotional temperature of the room is surprisingly honest and, by the end, what starts out as the tip of a man's life is suddenly this gargantuan reality rising up right in front of your eyes.

What's under the waterline? Stuff like:

- Four months ago my marriage ended because my wife's feelings were dead.
- I had an affair that devastated my marriage.
- I've destroyed the spirit and confidence of my wife and three kids by belittling, criticizing, and blaming them.
- I want to leave the 80/20 life and live 100 percent for God.
- I was so alone. Now I'm connected to some good men.

We are floating in an ocean of friends and acquaintances, co-workers, church fellowships, and tons of fraternities of men that only see our tips. These are the emotional truths men are keeping below the surface 24/7, and no one knows how influential these matters are to his life. The tragedy is that these problems lurking below produce a plethora of negative emotions. And left to our own devices, we will translate those emotions into unhealthy responses. These powerful feelings are the jagged edges that will shipwreck families, faith, and futures.

What's incredible is that male cultures worldwide are trained to accept just the tip, the visible surface of men, at the expense of the real substance of his life. We take what people say at face value, ask inch-deep questions and gladly rubber stamp an answer.

"How's it going, Tom?"

"Great, Larry."

We do it by habit, by culture. We're all too painfully absorbed in our own problems. It would drain too much emotional capital if we chose to go deeper. What would we have left for ourselves?

Dealing only with others' surfaces eliminates the very purpose of being connected to others in the first place. God intended us to help, redeem, equip, encourage, warn, and counsel our brothers as family, as good Samaritans. But instead, our discomfort with reality and lack of character proves our immaturity.

We can't act so surprised when a brother in our close-knit community does something that we term as scandal. How can we express shock at men's behavior when, if we're honest, there's no true relational basis there? What personal knowledge allows us to be shocked? Afterward, comments about The Scandal stem from a perceived image based on wafer-thin interactions like passing at the mailbox.

"I would have never expected him to do that. He seemed like such a nice guy."

The more honest thing to say would be, "I didn't know the guy at all." Sadly, this is still the case in many supposedly intimate circles of men— people presenting the tips of their lives in an acceptable context, and under the pretext of community. How amazing is it that we're afraid to probe deeper for fear of offending, and these men are bleeding right in front of us?

Jesus was not a man who accepted anybody's tip. He always worked to get below the waterline and help people accept the real issues. They were the issues preventing them from experiencing His best for their lives. If you want to be God's man and live out the character of the God-Man, you can't accept tips any longer either.

Gotcha!

Christlikeness is about looking past the exteriors of men and discerning what the big, emotional icebergs are in people's lives. When the Master went into action, He dug down.

The Woman at the Well

Everyone who drinks this water will be thirsty again, but whoever drinks the water I give him will never thirst. Indeed, the water I give him will become in him a spring of water welling up to eternal life. (John 4:13–14)

Thirsty? Kinda. Thirsty for intimacy with the God who sees all? Absolutely.

The Rich Young Ruler

"If you want to be perfect, go, sell your possessions and give to the poor, and you will have treasure in heaven. Then come, follow me." When the young man heard this, he went away sad, because he had great wealth. (Matthew 19:21–22)

Interested in becoming God's man? No thanks, I'll be a money man.

The Pharisees

"Why don't your disciples live according to the tradition of the elders instead of eating their food with 'unclean' hands?" He replied, "Isaiah was right when he prophesied about you hypocrites; as it is written: 'These people honor me with their lips, but their hearts are far from me. They worship me in vain; their teachings are but rules taught by men.' You have let go of the commands of God and are holding on to the traditions of men." (Mark 7:5–8)

Interested in pleasing God? Nope. Let's just keep things the way they are; it's so much more comfortable.

Martha

Martha opened her home to him. She had a sister called Mary, who sat at the Lord's feet listening to what he said. But Martha was distracted by all the preparations that had to be made. She came to him and asked, "Lord, don't you care that my sister has left me to do the work by myself? Tell her to help me!" "Martha, Martha," the Lord answered, "you are worried and upset about many things, but only one thing is needed. Mary has chosen what is better, and it will not be taken away from her." (Luke 10:38–42)

Was her sister really lazy? Or was Martha an anxious workaholic who chose worry and busyness over intimacy?

The Disciples

> Do not let your hearts be troubled. Trust in God; trust also in me.
> In my Father's house are many rooms; if it were not so, I would
> have told you. I am going there to prepare a place for you. And if I
> go and prepare a place for you, I will come back and take you to be
> with me that you also may be where I am. (John 14:1–3)

Was the room strangely silent because of the disciples' quiet confidence? Nope. Was anyone besides Peter expressing concern about Jesus's leaving? Nope. Was anybody a little mad about Jesus's statement, "Where I am going, you cannot follow now" (John 13:36)? Not visibly. But Jesus saw below the waterline, knowing they were terrified at the prospect of His leaving.

In the litany of Jesus's iceberg moments with people, these examples are just a fraction. He did this all the time. Jesus was simply not interested in the show, the presentation, or the justified or unjustified surface emotions of people. He had no taste for the symptoms; He went after the root. His

dream fact
God's man is simply not interested in surface image.

mission was to enter and redeem hearts, not to respond to disguises, diversions, or denial. His modus operandi worked off of what He knew about people: that we're all icebergs with deeper spiritual dramas unfolding below the waterline. The difference is that He would go there. He would do a heart scan rather than a behavioral assessment. With His unique heart sonar equipment, He took spiritual readings, constantly measuring the invisible. You see Him taking readings of hearts and people insisting on trying to distract Him with head tactics: goofy logic, stonewalling, dysfunctional reasoning, justification, defending, and desperately trying to draw attention away from the real heart problem. But each time, He would throw their x-ray film on the light board and expose the blockages. As a spiritual radiologist, Jesus would interpret what He saw. What did He see?

- hurts
- fears
- insecurities
- sin
- mixed motives
- lust
- wounds
- abandonment
- shame
- pride
- loss
- negative emotions à la carte

Jesus would intentionally go to where real pain, pride, or paranoia existed, because He knew that was where the potential for real spiritual change existed. Fact is, it's not that difficult to do. Jesus knew how human beings are wired. He knew exactly where to probe, what to look for, where to cut, where to remove a spiritual blockage, and how to introduce the healing process between the person and God.

He knew the place to be was below the waterline where all the spiritual action resided. He'd ask, "Does this hurt?" and He would get the reaction He was looking for—a response, positive or negative. You could not be a spiritual Switzerland, neutral about everything, while Jesus was around. That's how He meant it to be. When people responded, He had fulfilled His duty to His Father. He would touch the root issues fast and precipitate a response: a conscious choice to act.

Getting In

Jesus was very good at heart radiology. This also made Him the best connector ever to walk the planet. His eye was always on the ball in one-on-one interactions. His words and ways, His actions and attitudes, and His beliefs and behaviors indicated that He was always discerning, identifying and addressing the core issues preventing connections with his Father.

How did He go there, get there, stay there, and win for the kingdom, regardless of response? Watch Him and see. It was a little of this, a little of that, depending on the individual need.

Parables captivated, intrigued, and touched souls, often better than an announcement or a direct challenge could have. Progressively revealing questions allowed Him to slip below the waterline to people's issues. Sometimes He would appeal to familiar things to make analogies and prepare the soil for the seed to germinate understanding. Other times the need was so obvious (Martha, the disciples), He would simply go after the elephant in the room. How did He do it? He assessed a situation and allowed His superior insight to guide Him.

I often think it must have been nice to see right through the masks, disguises, motives, and defense tactics of everyone. He could go right for the spiritual juggler every time! In fairness, the Son of God was working with some advanced imaging technology. But He also lives inside us, hoping to give us that experience of scanning hearts and applying solutions. God's man, you are both equipped by the Holy Spirit and called by God to be a one-of-a-kind heart specialist. God's dream for you is this big: He wants you to become a heart doctor like Jesus.

Go back to the heart scans. An important tool in cardiology, MRI (magnetic resonance imaging) machines are especially helpful, not only in seeing the condition of the heart, but in evaluating the prescription for overall improved heart health. What makes this medical marvel irreplaceable is its ability to:

- see small structures or blockages
- peer into valves and chambers
- assess the overall structure and shape of the heart
- look directly at the coronary arteries feeding into the heart

It's all about detection. These scans reveal the size, shape, condition, and position of the heart, which is exactly what Jesus was after spiritually, to:

- see where the spiritual or emotional blockages were clogging someone's ability to believe
- peer into the valves and chambers of their experiences
- assess the overall structure of the character these experiences produced
- look directly at the truths or lies presently feeding into their beliefs about Him and His plan for their lives

Jesus took pictures. He showed what He saw. He identified core problems, and helped people see the picture of their problem. Then He offered Himself and His way as the solution. In the end, the patient chooses to accept the diagnosis or reject it—to pursue spiritual health or put it off for later.

Spiritual Cardiology 101

Jesus appreciated the fragility of the human heart. With great discernment, discretion, and love above all, He made it His aim to connect. In biblical terms, the heart represented a person's beliefs, passions, emotions, will, drives, ambitions, and desires—all the spiritual hard wiring.

Jesus knew this was what He was seeing—in painful, prideful, and fearful forms—below the waterline. The good news is that He wants to give you His ability to see those issues and help you be motivated to use that ability. This is real love. True discernment of people without Christ-centered love is not possible. Any other way and you have an agenda.

This is nonnegotiable in following Jesus's footsteps and becoming a good spiritual cardiologist. "And this is my prayer: that your love may abound more and more in knowledge and depth of insight, so that you may be able to discern what is best and may be pure and blameless until the day of Christ, filled with the fruit of righteousness that comes through Jesus Christ—to the glory and praise of God" (Philippians 1:9–11).

To love others in a meaningful way requires discernment, which, in turn, requires a good knowledge and understanding of people. A person's *gestalt* (gesh-TALT), the core thoughts and experiences, constitute who that person really is when integrated as a whole. This is as opposed to the outer personality or image someone projects. Jesus was great at nailing people's gestalt, and once He found a handle, He went for it. He could go there because He loved them deeply.

> **dream fact**
> *God gives you insight when the motives in your heart are pure.*

This is why for God's man there is a definite connection between deep, Christlike love for people and the insight God gives you into others.

Similarly, Jesus hugely disdained and chastised those with spiritual costumes who only pretended to care for people. They were clueless to the real needs in people's hearts because they loved themselves more than the people they were trying to help. The point is, why would God give any man insight into people if that man had mixed motives in his heart?

This spiritual skill also implies a clear ability to help others understand what really matters in life in order to integrate those core values into our lives. Our task as God's men in connecting with others is to be guided by love and an ability to see the important stuff, to discern. "What's that?" you ask. It means you care enough to know their heart issues and you're good at asking questions that connect to the heart. The biggies would be:

- family issues, past and present
- family losses
- other relationships
- personal core struggles and fears
- biggest hurts
- personality and wiring

See? It's not a long list. From the first century to the new millennium, people's core issues have not changed. These issues are the key indicators to test and probe. People who are able to get someone talking in these domains will get an up close and personal look into the chambers of the heart, and—it's a good bet—a response as well. This is where God wants you to go with people. His dream for you is not to be a good heart doctor, but to be a great one, like His Son.

When you care enough to search out the main issues of someone's heart, you become privy to who that person really is—his standards, ethics, motives, driving passions, and real gods. Like Jesus, you're called to train your recognition of the differences between appearances and reality, between public images and private struggles, between anger and hurt, pride and fear. God's man, like the God-Man, is ever growing in his abilities to scan for good and bad intentions, right and wrong agendas, healthy and unhealthy spiritual patterns, and the vital issues behind people's words, behaviors, and thoughts.

The great news is that we have the best teacher in the universe. He shows us the way into the heart. He prompts us as we study others. We can see His mind in the Scriptures, dialogue with Him, ask Him for discernment, listen for His voice, and respond to His direction. The skill comes as we seek to help the lost find their way to Him and ultimately to find their healing in Him.

In the end, it's difficult to conceal yourself from a discerning God's man. As Jesus strips away our defenses and replaces them with His acceptance and authority, we see ourselves and others more clearly. When a man's fears have been defeated by love, there's no pretending. That's when they see Him—in you. They just can't fake it when Jesus, the seer of hearts, is in the house. You are a heart doc, a seer beneath the surface, a submariner.

And when you are in real relationship like this, they'll be aware that *someone else* is aware of what's below.

Now get out there and dive! Dive! Dive!

chapter 11

velvet touch

There are only two kinds of men: the righteous who think they are sinners and the sinners who think they are righteous.

—BLAISE PASCAL

Their spiritual processors could not run the "Jesus application." Their programs just couldn't recognize a man who made it a habit to connect with the sexually immoral, physically unclean, and ethnically impure.

This would often send the religious leaders' spiritual hard drives into a system overload as they desperately tried to make sense of Him. The ease with which He floated from the temple to the countryside, from the synagogue to the sinners' districts, raised eyebrows and ignited plenty of gossip. He broke their rules about first- and second-class citizens. He was not acting "righteous" in His associations. His credibility as a spiritual leader was eroded by His dubious itinerary. The Father, on the other hand, was rejoicing saying, "That's the way, Son! Exactly!" God's Son was moving the kingdom forward not just in shady back alleys of first-century Palestine but also in every other place where those starving for acceptance were found.

The lost were being found. The "found" just got more lost.

Jesus did not blend with contemporary religious expression simply because He made His grace available to all. To be this way, He could not be codependent with culture, racial caricature, tradition, or the pseudoholy practices of exclusion. To deliver God's grace on earth, the criteria was this: honest need. When He found this, He would jump in the boat and make it over to that person's shore. "Jesus unplugged" is a story of grace in motion—dangerously attractive, inviting, and controversial. And God's dream for us is that we be the same.

> ### dream fact
> *God's dream for us is dangerously attractive, inviting, and controversial.*

If you are like me, you have to let go of your fears and let Jesus take over. I am not a radical, go-out-of-my-way connector, especially with people not like me. I much prefer sanitized and tidy. But that's not going to cut it. I must study Him, watch Him, and seek to agent His grace. When I look closely at the Gospels, I'm convicted, because what I see is that nothing stopped the God-Man from affirming and accepting excluded people. He went to them and they went to Him. In every case, grace and people collided beautifully.

I want the excluded to feel Him when they collide with me.

Pure Grace

Reject or accept. Avoid or engage. Steer clear or draw near. Pass over or pick out.

This is the language of exclusion and inclusion. Think junior high. Think picking teams on the playground as a little boy. The emotions there were real and raw. I don't know who makes it onto your private quarantine list, maybe a homosexual co-worker, an obese neighbor, an alcoholic uncle, your "out there" son-in-law, but just think of someone you shy away from. Why are you afraid? Why do they give you a fever emotionally? How has God called you to relate to them?

Jesus Accepted the Physically Unacceptable

While Jesus was in one of the towns, a man came along who was covered with leprosy. When he saw Jesus, he fell with his face to the ground and begged him, "Lord, if you are willing, you can make me clean." Jesus reached out his hand and touched the man. "I am willing," he said. "Be clean!" And immediately the leprosy left him. (Luke 5:12–13)

Think of a forgotten dish in the back of your refrigerator that's been there for a few weeks. It's gone bad, covered with fuzzy mold. Think about your reaction when you lift the foil. Did you make a face? This man—this leper—was visibly shocking from a physical perspective. Imagine a man covered with leprosy. Got it? Your natural reaction to this human mold would probably be the same—your face would contort and you would recoil. That's what this man experienced on a daily basis in first-century Palestine. He was so ashamed of his appearance he could not look Jesus in the face. Ask yourself, *What is a man with leprosy most hungry for?*

Now look at what the God-Man gave him first and you have found your answer. Notice He didn't heal him physically first. He touched him! Imagine you are this man and you see Jesus. He comes up to you, reaching out, about to do the unthinkable. *Is He extending his arm? No! No, Lord!* And then He does it anyway. Imagine that touch. Just imagine it: you haven't experienced positive human touch in years, maybe decades, and then Jesus's hand makes contact with your shoulder. For you, that touch is the grace of God. Touch is acceptance; touch is affirmation of dignity. Jesus is healing your heart and saving you simply by His touch. The grace of God is pouring over you and not a word has been said.

> No! No, Lord! *And then He does it anyway.*

Notice here that Jesus's first communication does not produce the physical healing. It proves the acceptance of this person. He is worth healing. What must have been flowing through the leprous man's head upon feeling that mighty touch of acceptance? And then to hear the words "I am willing." I can see eyes locking in a silent acknowledgment between them. The message is simple: "You are not alone, my brother." Ten megatons of grace detonated in that man's heart. After that, the physical healing was just the mushroom cloud following the internal explosion.

Jesus Accepted the Morally Unacceptable

Now one of the Pharisees invited Jesus to have dinner with him, so he went to the Pharisee's house and reclined at the table. When a woman who had lived a sinful life in that town learned that Jesus was eating at the Pharisee's house, she brought an alabaster jar of perfume, and as she stood behind him at his feet weeping, she began to wet his feet with her tears. Then she wiped them with her hair, kissed them and poured perfume on them. When the Pharisee who had invited him saw this, he said to himself, "If this man were a prophet, he would know who is touching him and what kind of woman she is—that she is a sinner." (Luke 7:36–39)

Most Christians have a hard time separating the sin and the sinner. Jesus did not. He didn't make the distinction between outward sins and the less visible sins of the heart.

Adultery and lust of the heart looked the same to Jesus, whereas men would draw the distinction, or at least be unaware of the hidden one. In Jesus's mind, every person reclining at that table was just like this woman! The problem was that they did not see themselves the way Jesus saw them. Jesus would lump them in the same boat with this woman— sinners needing to be sanctified—while they drew distinctions and labels out of pride and a fear of connecting. This mental division between people leads to thoughts and actions that are beyond arrogant and headed toward evil. And all this came from the supposedly spiritual men at the table!

Imagine the scene. This woman had probably heard Jesus preach and, having a new hope and change of heart, she determined to live a new life. So she comes to the table, presents herself (her gender another stigma in a group of first-century religious men), and offers worship out of love and gratitude. The smell of her shame transforms into the perfume of acceptance, and that acceptance is filling the air of that room. Such acceptance, instead of smelling sweet to these religious men, produces tension and resistance. Jesus can smell it instantly, and He doesn't like the odor. So he redresses the man publicly: "I tell you, her many sins have been forgiven—for she loved much. But he who has been forgiven little loves little" (Luke 7:47). In other words: she gets Me. You don't. She knows she is a sinner. You don't know that you are. Her love is evidence of her forgiveness. Your ambivalence toward her and Me shows you've yet to understand it.

Jesus Accepted the Ethnically Unacceptable

> Now he had to go through Samaria.... When a Samaritan woman came to draw water, Jesus said to her, "Will you give me a drink?" (His disciples had gone into the town to buy food.) The Samaritan woman said to him, "You are a Jew and I am a Samaritan woman. How can you ask me for a drink?" (For Jews do not associate with Samaritans.) Jesus answered her, "If you knew the gift of God and who it is that asks you for a drink, you would have asked him and he would have given you living water." (John 4:4, 7–10)

Samaritans were perceived as an ethnic malfunction in Jesus's day—a blight which reminded the Jews of a season in their history they would rather forget. Samaritans were the product of interracial bloodlines formed during the forced exile in Babylon—a racial amalgam despised by the ethnically pure. Jews, especially the spiritual ones, wanting to get to Galilee from Judea would cross over to the east side of the Jordan, and walk around Samaria to avoid being tainted by the bad blood. This custom reinforced the racism and preserved standards of ceremonial cleanliness. So when we see Jesus intentionally planning to go through Samaria, we see the God-Man with matches in His hand, intending to light a fuse that will explode the cultural boundaries of His day.

Now look at the reaction from the woman at His request. She's obviously uncomfortable. "This isn't right. Don't you know better?" Then, just in case He's plain ignorant, she informs Him of the rules governing this infraction. "Don't you see that ethnic roadside bomb your foot is about to step on?" But Jesus gets right to heart of the matter: "I'm not your average Jew, and this is not your average request."

The "gift of God" he talks about is nothing less than the grace and acceptance of God through Christ. It's a bridge that's difficult for her to cross. She's trying to create separation, and Jesus is moving the conversation toward connection. She's trying to feel properly offended in line with her cultural roots, but Jesus is trying offer her life in line with His kingdom roots. She's thinking, *Well, this is new.*

> *"This isn't right. Don't you know better?"*

And then the disciples return, find these two engaged in conversation, and are caught off guard at the cultural and gender boundary infraction the Master is "Samarily" dismissing. Can't you see it? A bunch of traditional Jewish men raised to avoid Samaritans, asking one another, "Is that Jesus over there? What in Sam-Harry-huh is He doing?" Their second thought might have been more private: *What is this going to mean for us?*

These are the natural questions for a disciple to ask.

Latter Day Leper

John Forbes's dad drank. If you are the son of an alcoholic, like me, you can probably guess that his dad was closer with the local liquor storeowners than with him. John emotionally pursued his dad for years,

but it was like chasing the wind—always elusive and ultimately disappointing. He was a figment, a phantom.

As the years passed, little John grew into a bigger, man-size John. Now he
had man-size issues, man-size responsibilities, and a monster-size hole in
his heart. This wound was a black hole sucking every particle of attention
and affirmation into its gravitational void, crushing anyone who got too
close. It could not be filled. The little boy heart inside that big body
sought one desperate question: can you prove I am worthy of love?

He searched in vain for someone who could answer that question. This
unfulfilled longing would eventually be filled by other men: ones who
would accept and affirm, ones who would physically touch, ones who
would give him their time and talk, ones who couldn't wait to see him
come through the door. They were not his dad but they were there to
pretend—temporarily. Other men try other things—the vices don't matter; it's whatever offers relief, however temporary.

John became a follower of Jesus Christ after he'd fallen deep into his
emotional and sexual tailspin. The lost boy had been found. New hope
invaded his soul. The highest of these hopes included being able to deal
directly with a broken sexual identity, engage in this new spiritual journey
and invest his energies for Christ. He made great strides, but it would
always be tempered by the voice inside, seizing his mind with the old
ways, laying out the old succulent feast of indulgences.

During seasons of emotional famine, these temptations were hard to resist.
John fought the urges, life would overwhelm, and the voices inside and
out would press harder. Slowly and steadily, the old John began to prevail,

quickly eroding his eight years of following Christ. His new convictions faltered. His first love was lost. John gave up and gave in to the voices. But instead of finding the old simple pleasures, he found crushing spiritual doubt and self-loathing. In his own words, "I thought Jesus could deliver me from a homosexual life! What does that mean?" Satan whispers, *You were never delivered, because you can't be. It's who you are.*

The next three years were a spiritual Vietnam for John Forbes. Christian friends were sympathetic, but afraid. Many were unhelpful or ashamed of his struggle, creating even more spiritual disillusionment and doubt. Even pastors couldn't engage him meaningfully, yielding instead to fear, applying quick fixes, and eventually giving up. Alienated from the body of Christ, John's insecurities grew more powerful. Rational lies previously rejected were now more appealing and easily spun into justifications, even entitlements to dive back into sin. It was just a matter of time before opportunities knocked.

The polluted reasoning led to a full embrace of the old John. He found himself standing in front of a wardrobe closet he

> *Satan whispers,* You were never delivered, because you can't be. It's who you are.

thought he would never reenter. John Forbes was going to put on "the old self and its practices" just like it talks about in the Bible. His exodus was over; he was going back to Egypt. The old identities were put on, the old loyalties accommodated, relationships reunited, behaviors revisited. Even though these old clothes didn't fit the same way, they were familiar.

John began a season of wild temporary thrills accessorized by alcohol, cocaine, and homosexual liaisons, but this time there was no freedom.

Deep down, John knew the old ways represented a default existence produced by spiritual desperation. Yet he denied the reality hundreds of times, in hundreds of moments, amidst thousands of experiences over the next eight years.

Until finally, the season of kicks was met by the ultimate kickback.

Dirty

In addition to feeling far beyond the borders of God's grace after eight years back in his Egypt, John started feeling ill. The unrelenting coldlike symptoms and blood in his urine landed him in an examination room. That stark room was a contrast to the new life the old John had tried to rebuild. For a man so privately fragmented and empty, his life as a producer in New York and Europe, along with other prestigious work in theater, plus influence, affluence, and buckets of affirmation, John appeared quite together. Yet at this moment, the public image stood in direct contrast to the sterile reality that faced him: waiting to walk through the door.

Then the door opened.

"Mr. Forbes, I am sorry to inform you that you have tested positive for HIV."

What?

Like a shell-shocked soldier trying to regain his senses after being knocked over by the force of an exploding bomb, John could not hear, think, or feel. The doctor's lips kept moving, but the rippling vertigo prevented assimilation. Numbing minutes ticked by until, finally, a thought snapped him out of the trance. *Work! I need to get to work!*

The little visit over, he exited the building onto the streets of Manhattan, one hundred and fifty dollars poorer. A sickening price for this sickening dose of reality. *Thanks for what?* He closed his checkbook and wandered the streets, slowly feeling the tears turning to sobs. Crushing thought after thought came unbidden. He was almost certain that the Lord was punishing him for his sinful behavior. *How did it come to this? My life has become a spiritual satire.*

In the days following his diagnosis, attempts were made to reconnect with God, church, and Christians. His own insecurities about sharing his news, combined with awkward responses served only to further exacerbate the pain. Christ followers piled on even more sickness:

- judgment
- hostility
- phobic behavior
- tense pseudohugs

And all of it with the unspoken but pervasive message: *You are dirty.*

His worst fears were being realized. The clear rejection only magnified his crushing sense of regret, helplessness, and insignificance.

Where now? John did the math:

- Dirty meant untouchable.
- Untouchable meant unlovable.
- Unlovable meant worthless.
- Worthless meant his life didn't matter.
- If his life didn't matter, he might as well throw it away.

Cocaine binges gave way to a crack addiction and alcohol binges for days on end. If he was dirty, he figured he might as well act like it.

God's people had rejected him. However, Jesus had not. And through an unusual encounter, John's doubts, fears, shame, and ugliness were overcome, overwhelmed by a divine acceptance he'd never known—and one he'd never quite be able to shake:

> In a moment of revelation, I saw the Lord on his throne and me approaching him. I just began to weep. I became aware of God's love for me at that moment. Not with head knowledge but with an incredible sense of his presence. It overwhelmed me. I could not stop crying. God really is gracious and compassionate, slow to anger and abounding in love—he doesn't treat us as our sins deserve. After all I had done, I was still met with his mercy.
>
> Since developing AIDS in 2001, and that encounter with the Lord, things have radically turned around for me. The Lord has firmly established me in his truth and love. I am growing in grace and the knowledge of that love. It is transforming the deepest part of me. I know him. He is restoring my physical health. He took an alcoholic and a drug addict with AIDS and opened up opportunities for me to share his love all over the world.[4]

This is how Jesus engages "dirty."

Jesus engaged dirty with velvety grace—the soft, comforting touch of His acceptance. He blanketed the shame, overlooked the ugliness, and utterly conquered the stigma with His presence. He eliminated the possibility of rejection and replaced it with participation. He obliterated the need to keep secrets and hide. The failures of men were replaced by unfailing love—full rejection replaced by full acceptance. That's what Jesus does with an HIV-positive man in America.

It's what we would expect to hear. It would layer nicely into Matthew, Mark, Luke, or John. It preaches well. But in practice, it should convict us to our souls, the same way the parable of the good Samaritan disturbed the religious guys in Jesus's day. He deliberately placed a priest and a Levite in the story to "out" them as bankrupt God's men. Similarly, John Forbes's story confronts everyone who plays spiritual. John was in theater, but the ones really acting were the ones dressed in Christian clothes and putting on airs. Jesus thrived with the dirty and the ragamuffins of His culture.

I am not sure we do. And none of us is excused.

Why is it that so much is said about grace while so few of us give it away? A simple presence, an embrace and acceptance moves the prodigals back in the right direction. Yet instead of having a soft spot for sinners, we're terrified of them. Generally, the message we send is that the saints don't need the sinners. It's a good thing Jesus didn't feel the same. "The Son of Man came eating and drinking, and they say, 'Here is a glutton and a drunkard, a friend of tax collectors and "sinners"'" (Matthew 11:19).

The only times we see Jesus build a wall with people was when their pride had blinded them to the reality of their own need. In those rare instances, He traded the velvet touch of grace for a steel hammer of truth (we'll explore this aspect in the next chapter). But if critics accused Jesus of being comfortable with sinners, what makes us assume they won't be just as offended by us? Christ followers should be really good at offending these types.

dream fact

If critics accused Jesus of consorting with sinners, they'll be just as offended by us.

Expressing God's grace. Allowing the Holy Spirit to use us to help others feel God's acceptance. Having faith and the courage to affirm people apart from their sin. These are the velvet responses most needed by those who believe they're beyond the Father's love.

"The Word became flesh and made his dwelling among us. We have seen his glory, the glory of the One and Only, who came from the Father, full of grace and truth" (John 1:14). Jesus—the Word in the flesh—was the ambassador of God's grace. We cannot compartmentalize this most radical and transforming aspect of Jesus's character. We can't separate it from our journey as God's man.

Jesus was generous in His acceptance. His unequivocal desire is for His men to be good at it too.

Self or Others?

Are you self-effacing or self-important?

Zacchaeus was physically and ethically unacceptable. Yet Jesus wanted him to experience God's acceptance. The crippled woman was spiritually unacceptable as a Gentile, but that didn't stop Jesus from accepting and healing her. Children were nuisances to busy rabbis, but Jesus said, "Let the little children come" (Matthew 19:14). Even from the cross, Jesus was asking the Father to forgive and accept His crucifiers. All this acceptance of those people was culturally counterintuitive. It was radical. To play by God's rules, the Son of God had to break man's rules.

Who is more deserving of the grace of God? No one.

Some people's baselines of acceptance are based on behaviors, appearances, and cultural biases. The religious men of Jesus's time held ethnic prejudices and masked them in spiritual requirements. Their filter was broken. This was how they saw others, which reflected how they saw themselves. And then there was how Jesus saw them and how that reflected His identity. Their views of themselves were culturally guided, which polluted their ability to extend God's grace. This only contributed to more wounding.

Even us—when we see others under oppressive shame, the sinfulness in us loves that we are better than they are. The folly is that we fail to see ourselves in them.

Who do you have difficulty loving as Jesus did? You don't necessarily need to love their behavior or image, but what prevents you from seeing them as a person Christ died for and wants to help? Could it be that God has put them in your life for you to touch? Could it be that Jesus wants to use them to put you in closer touch with Him? Could it be that He wants to show you the lengths He went to accept you, to make you grateful?

Think about it. The bottom line is this: Jesus Christ embraced the unacceptable and condemned the spiritual people who shunned them.

What does that say about God's people who rejected John Forbes? This reality of who Jesus is gives me pause—a long sobering, reflective, and convicting one. He associated with the social outcasts as easily as He connected with the religious. Wherever sinners found a tongue to engage Him honestly, they would find heaven ready to meet them with open arms. That's right; the startling fact about Jesus was this: *His standards were quite low.* That is why God's man, regardless of his station in life, should be the freer one among men to engage others without borders and walls.

> **dream fact**
> *Jesus Christ embraced the unacceptable.*

All of our ability and insight into being an agent of grace in the lives of others hinges on how you answer one question: are you self-effacing or self-important? Only one identity preserves the dignity of others. Only one tears down the walls of separation. Only one conquers culture to connect. Only one of these creates a soft spot for the unacceptable. Only one loves "dirty." Only one overcomes appearances. Only one identity connects with the shameful, allows personal pain and convinces the undeserving they are not beyond the reach of acceptance. Only one possesses a velvet touch.

Only one identity sees grace and gives grace away as freely as it was received. Only one can realize the dream.

To learn more about John Forbes and his ministry, visit www.agapeincintl.org.

chapter 12

bullish on reality

When you argue with reality, you lose—but only 100 percent of the time.

—BYRON KATIE

Reality (n): not the way we wish things to be, nor the way they appear, but the way things actually are.

Jesus was big on reality.

Sounds cliché, but when you study Him, the words He speaks, and His interactions with men, you see that He wanted people to possess the truth no matter the cost.

In this sense I am so unlike Him. I lie naturally. I cover up naturally. I don't want people to be mad at me. I want to be accepted. I want people to feel good. I don't want to hurt others. My character can disintegrate in these hard realities—it gets exposed. My courage to face, speak, live out, and integrate the whole truth about my flaws is difficult without His spine in me, holding me up.

Thank God for His backbone.

Being God's man means being a man whose character is centered in the true reality. *Versus what?* you ask. Versus being a man centered on appearances. Perceptions. Rationalizations. Deceits. Fantasies. Self-deceptions and all other shades of unreality. Christlikeness is measured by a consistent acceptance of reality—especially when it hurts. How do I know? Because this is the essence of the God-Man. The velvet touch of His grace is seamlessly paired with this indestructible commitment to truth. They are the two parts of His character that bring healing and health to all He touches. It's where the warmth of His unconditional acceptance intersects with the steel of accountability—affirmation meets authority. It's what gets me into relationship with God and what transforms me into someone different. It is the anointed dynamic of God's grace loving me while His truth transforms me. Grace feels like a comfortable hug. Truth feels like a swift slap to the backside.

Yet both show love.

When I take bold steps toward painful realities, I know it is Jesus in me and not myself. How do I know? First, because it's not my natural pattern. I prefer comfort. I prefer safe fantasy. Second, because Jesus did not spin the facts when there was a risk of loss or a potentially negative consequence. In fact, he leaned in harder when there was a risk of people believing fantasies. Did this make Jesus a wet rag? Sometimes. No one likes their parade rained on. But when our parade gets out of control, the truth of our circumstances can be a refreshing rain.

I see this reality fudging going on all the time in men's ministry, especially when husbands have grown deeply afraid of reality and lead their wives to believe some sort of falsehood. I see it in pastors unwilling to share their dark sides of struggle with temptation because of the pedestal effect—when the pressure of popularity puts them in a prison of pomposity and self-preservation. I see it when men are unable to accept the brutal facts surrounding lust and fantasy and its lasting impact on relationships. I see it in superficial male relationships—guys bleeding right in front in their buddies' eyes.

And still we're surprised when one of these men takes his own life after leaving a note that explains the loneliness that led to his hopelessness. I have attended such funerals. And for what? We think we're at risk of losing our image, prestige, or control. Or more to the pain of the point, we spin reality to avoid a consequence that will unload a magazine of negative emotions into our lives. Both patterns wind up creating significantly bigger problems than a little discomfort up front.

> **dream fact**
> *Christlikeness is measured by how much reality you accept.*

All of this emotional cloak and dagger, fear and pride, denial and neglect turns Jesus's stomach and breaks His heart. We have all these fears of reality in the areas where our pride gets bruised. That pride causes us to fear potential pain and waste our energy on paranoia, wanting our lives to make sense and fit a certain perception. And when life, relationships, or circumstances don't fit the self-image we're seeking to create, we mess with reality just enough to keep the mask on. With this man, his reality is usually more dubious and dark than his report. He's living in fantasy. But just because he's stopped believing in reality doesn't mean it goes away. In fact, the reality has grown stronger and more insidious inside him. Why? Because Christ is losing and the impostor is winning.

The solution? Accept reality. Work with Jesus. Stop running.

> This is the crisis we're in: God-light streamed into the world, but men and women everywhere ran for the darkness. They went for the darkness because they were not really interested in pleasing God. Everyone who makes a practice of doing evil, addicted to denial and illusion, hates God-light and won't come near it, fearing a painful exposure. But anyone working and living in truth and reality welcomes God-light so the work can be seen for the God-work it is. (John 3:19–21, MSG)

This is what new birth as a man will look and feel like. The light of Christ shines into the secret places and exposes realities in our lives, the gaps He would like to help us fill. A full exposure to His light in our lives is the bright kind, leaving no corner unilluminated and leaving us exposed morally, emotionally, relationally, and spiritually. And though being exposed can be uncomfortable, Jesus insists this is a benevolent capture. In fact, running only precedes what will eventually be even worse when it is caught and exposed. We can choose to bolt back into the pseudoanonymity of the darkness to alleviate the present discomfort of exposure to reality. But we'll be so much better off welcoming the Holy Spirit's perfectly targeted conviction of a problem.

We should surrender to the Master Craftsman's loving pursuit of truth for us so He can finish His shaping work.

But why so much reality? Why the discomfort? Why the pushing and prodding to negotiate with the truth if it's there anyway? It's just the same truth that's always been there, right? It's not going anywhere. Why not just accept a little fantasy with your reality?

Jesus confronts all men with the facts, because anything less on His side makes Him a fraud and makes you not a brother, but an object of judgment. Holding to your fantasy makes you a recipient of His justice.

Reality Bites!

I am not your easy-going soccer dad. I freely admit that I can be one of those extreme dads who raises eyebrows at times. It can get so embarrassing at some games, I wonder if I need counseling. But before you start painting the mental picture of me pouncing on every whistle, chewing up refs, and spitting out opinions on game strategy, hear me out. That's not quite me. In fact, I've coached so many games, played so much soccer, and seen so many bad calls, I don't have the emotional energy to oppose every little thing. You can probably tell I'm trying to paint myself in a better light. I don't want you to lump me in with *that* kind of dad, the real crazies. But I can occasionally get a little out there in my antics. I definitely belong to the crazy dad fraternity at times. But go with my little story here anyway.

It was a cold Saturday morning. Cara was uncharacteristically prepared: clean, dressed, and ready to drive to the field at 6:15 a.m. I was up too, dressed and getting excited. Maybe a little too excited....

In a few minutes my daughter's team would meet the only other undefeated team in her division in a game that would determine who would win their twelve-team pool. The winner would be promoted to the super-elite premier division next year. They had steadily climbed through five lower divisions in recent years and were standing on the verge of achieving a dream few actually achieve—playing at the highest level. And this was not just another team they were playing today; this was Cara's old team, the one she left under some less-than-happy circumstances a few years earlier. The parents had been pumping up for this match-up all year, and we had circled this game on the calendar months ago, hoping for this exact dream scenario.

We arrived at the field, and I deposited Cara to join her team, parked the car, and entered the arena of "parental flatulation." There was a lot of emotional gas spilling out on our sideline, replete with insider gossip about the other coach and how he tried to recruit our players, and hearsay about certain players, etc., etc. The atmosphere was positively charged, and when the whistle blew, so did the maturity on both sidelines, including "Pastor Kenny's." Every call from the refs was hotly scorned, every hair-raising foul either lamented or overcelebrated, every shift in play screamed about mercilessly. And in the end, Cara's team ended up winning, 2–1.

> *The parents had been pumping up for this match-up all year.*

End of story right?

Wrong. I hadn't yet gotten my big healthy bite of reality. The following Wednesday at work, my phone rang and my assistant, Babbett, said, "A 'Carver' on the line for you." My first thought was: *I am toast. Grab your sackcloth and ashes. Prepare to deflate ego.* I reluctantly answered and my good friend Carver began with, "Kenny, you have put me in an awkward situation here." I knew where he was going. For the next twenty minutes, I took it. It was painful. I was an idiot the day of the game, and I let my competitive juices run roughshod over my best intentions. I had not held it together well.

While I didn't anticipate my friend to be nearly so gracious with me about my actions that Saturday, I knew I was receiving valuable reproof from a caring brother. Carver has known me since my UCLA days and attends my weekly men's Bible study at Saddleback. He wasn't afraid to deliver a little dose of reality to my front porch, even if his stepdaughter is on the other team. Here was a guy who knew that my number one strength and my number one weakness is my competitive nature. Under the control of the Holy Spirit, it can be a great thing, competing in the spiritual arenas of life, battling against sin, and fighting for the good stuff. Yet out of control, it leads to oppression. That's the downside—you make people feel like losers instead of being a gracious winner and a good sport.

Needless to say, it can be horrible for relationships. This game triggered the dark side and I was blind to it. Thank God Carver was not. Carver prayed, picked up his phone, and made a very nerve-racking call. Had he not, I would never have come face to face with the reality of my actions, my sin, and experienced the renewing power of repentance. I asked Carver if

dream fact
God's man channels his aggressive personality.

there was anyone he felt I should call or talk to. I apologized and confessed how I'm working on this area away from the soccer field as well. And again, he was gracious.

Talk about holy embarrassment. Reality bites—and leaves a mark! Carver sliced me off a good-sized bite, but he didn't intend me to suffer alone. It was a serving intended to satisfy—a morsel from a faithful friend. I needed to stop fooling myself about my actions and face the fact that I can be oppressive with my words. Chrissy appreciated the bite as well, since I had ignored her attempts to serve me some of the same dish. Now, as Churchill said, "The truth is incontrovertible, malice may attack it and ignorance may deride it, but, in the end, there it is." And truly, there it was, and I couldn't deny or deflect it. No excusing myself before I'd swallowed. Pure, unadulterated reality had come to me, and I was better for it. I could have spit it back in his face, but thank God I was not that foolish.

Taking Off the Gloves

Jesus, being the embodiment of all truth, knew the consequences of deceit with precise intuition. That's why God's dream for us to be like Christ includes the trait of authenticity—to permit reality and truth to guide our actions. When it came to matters of reality, He wasn't shy or composed when the situation demanded it. Jesus inhaled the present realities as He engaged people and circumstances, and He exhaled truth to address them. Just look at the ways that He suggested we allow reality to interface with our character:

Reality and Temptation

"If your hand causes you to sin, cut it off. It is better for you to enter life maimed than with two hands to go into hell" (Mark 9:43). The hard truth: amputate sin like a cancer. Be ruthless with it and unapologetic. If you don't, it will metastasize to come back, fester, and eventually kill you. That's a certainty.

Reality and God's Commands

"Why do you call me, 'Lord, Lord,' and do not do what I say?" (Luke 6:46). The hard truth: spiritual actions speak far louder than words. They are the ultimate marker of spiritual integrity. If you love someone, you seek alignment of your life to their priorities. Think about that. That's a real relationship. Anything else is fantasy.

Reality and Spiritual Deception

"You have heard that it was said, 'Do not commit adultery.' But I tell you that anyone who looks at a woman lustfully has already committed adultery with her in his heart" (Matthew 5:27–28). The hard truth: thoughts, motives, and intentions reveal who we really are, and behaviors only confirm it. The tip of the iceberg is what people see. The mass below the waterline is what God sees. So you can quit acting righteous and start being righteous.

Reality and Expectations

"I have told you these things, so that in me you may have peace. In this world you will have trouble. But take heart! I have overcome the world" (John 16:33). The hard truth: earth is not heaven; we should expect loss and grief. Yet we should anticipate God's redeeming our grief and fulfilling His purpose in it. Though full redemption of suffering may not come in this lifetime, earth's worst cannot escape God's best.

Reality and Spiritual Practice

"You hypocrites! Isaiah was right when he prophesied about you: 'These people honor me with their lips, but their hearts are far from me' " (Matthew 15:7–8). The hard truth: the motions might be right, but if the motivations are out of alignment, you might as well drop the charade. Playing church is playing with fire.

Reality and Loss

"When Jesus saw her weeping, and the Jews who had come along with her also weeping, he was deeply moved in spirit and troubled. 'Where have you laid him?' he asked. 'Come and see, Lord,' they replied. Jesus wept" (John 11:33–35). The hard truth: we are made to feel pain, not brush it off as someone else's misery. Jesus did not deny or try to fix the real loss of others in the moment. He experienced and connected with it. Anything less is out of touch with reality.

Reality and Emotional Isolation

"Come to me, all you who are weary and burdened, and I will give you rest" (Matthew 11:28). The hard truth: there is no such thing as emotionally satisfying self-sufficiency. There is only One with unlimited emotional resources—and you are not Him.

Reality and Persecution

" 'No servant is greater than his master.' If they persecuted me, they will persecute you" (John 15:20). The hard truth: a relationship with Jesus Christ involves suffering. Sign me up! It's just like Jesus to keep it real even if it means fewer numbers.

Reality and Dysfunction

" 'Martha, Martha,' the Lord answered, 'you are worried and upset about many things, but only one thing is needed. Mary has chosen what is better, and it will not be taken away from her' " (Luke 10:41–42). The hard truth: He accepts us as we are but loves us too much to leave us the way we are. Oh man, that's awkward, but it's a necessary part of reality and loving someone to health.

Reality and Secrets

" 'Go, call your husband and come back.' 'I have no husband,' she replied. Jesus said to her, 'You are right when you say you have no husband. The fact is, you have had five husbands, and the man you now have is not your husband. What you have just said is quite true' " (John 4:16–18). The hard truth: Jesus has seen our movie—every frame. Nothing is lost in translation here. Jesus knows all the facts about our dark spaces. That is either terrifying or quite relieving. Now we don't have to pretend or hide anything. It's for us, not Him.

Reality and Eternity

"In my Father's house are many rooms; if it were not so, I would have told you. I am going there to prepare a place for you" (John 14:2). The wonderful truth: we are never going to be separated—ever! This is the best reality of all.

Living in Reality

How does God's man know his character is becoming more like Christ's—more rooted in truth, in reality? For God's man it is the difference between the Old You and the New You—the Christ-formed one. The Christ-led man negotiates and lives in reality well. He is able to speak the truth, acknowledge the truth in a situation, and encourage others to face reality with a truthful perspective. He's learned that the emotionally convenient and comfortable response is often the misleading one. He is guided by the Holy Spirit's strong leadership, and finds truth in reality. When this happens, plenty more good stuff comes about in God's man. He:

- accepts responsibility and evaluates his shortcomings
- seeks constructive feedback from others and embraces consequences
- acknowledges and deals with negative emotions versus swallowing them
- makes the hard (and better) call early
- doesn't hide from losses and hurts, but grieves them
- stops blaming others to cover for his mistakes
- stops seeking affirmation to compensate for insecurity
- speaks up with others, to them, and for them when the Holy Spirit prompts

This is the life I guard vigilantly with a Sherman tank. It is the precious way of living that Jesus has imparted to me, ten times more liberating than any alternatives. It's the life of seeing things as they really are and trusting God for how it will be. It's the life that doesn't have to fit a perception. It bears fruit in eagerly consenting to reality rather than resenting or reluctantly accepting it. It convicts and excites me by operating on the principle that action and engagement is better, and silence is a temptation from the Enemy. It's the life that knows denial is my greatest adversary and acceptance of truth is my greatest ally.

This is the life that has stopped being selective about the parts of reality I accept due to fear or pride.

Are you there yet? Or are you still selective about the reality you accept? What are you not able to confront yet? What is the big, fat hairy elephant in the space of your life? Is God big enough to handle your truth? Does He have enough love to cover it? Does He have enough power and purpose to transform it? These are the questions which lead you to be like Christ—putting you in touch with reality and truth, versus cultivating more fantasy. One life is authentic and feels real. The other is synthetic and feels superficial.

What does authenticity feel like? Every "aha" moment, every, "Whoa, that's deep!" and every, "*Now* I see," is the result of His work in your life. Jesus Christ takes full credit for all truth, all moments of revelation, and all experiences with the awesome scope of reality working in and through our lives. In fact, any realization leading to greater awareness of truth and godliness has His imprint on it. Similarly, God cannot affirm or bless our rejection of truth. The declaration, "I am…the truth," automatically infers an equal and diametrically opposite declaration by Christ which is, "I am *not* deception." The point is, God's man thinks twice every time he is tempted to entertain harmful thoughts. What does synthetic and superficial feel like? Slimy. It just doesn't ring true or feel true.

- *This won't hurt anybody.*
- *God will understand this one time.*
- *God wouldn't want me to live like this.*
- *He'll forgive me.*

Rationalizing is the opposite of reality. Excusing ourselves from the reality of our responsibility as God's man will not be accepted. Those things don't fly. They are not

dream fact
Denial is our greatest adversary, and acceptance of truth is our greatest ally.

Christlike. Your awareness of His love for you, Christ's character forming in you, and your partnership with the Holy Spirit inside incinerates such self-deception. More important, God's man knows that the acceptance or promotion of a lie produces great negative consequences. Acknowledgment and acceptance, no matter how painful, produce the greatest freedoms and blessings in life.

To be like Christ, the gloves must come off. It's time to see, engage, and interact with what *is,* not what you wish it was. It takes a man-sized courage to live in truth and reality—you must be open to personal transformation.

The hard part? Admitting your identity and your energies may have been partially misplaced. But you have the opportunity today to become more like Christ—a man who doesn't have to create a world of unreality to make himself feel better or more secure.

The bottom line is that Jesus negotiates reality very well. He should—He created it. And that means that the One living in you is just waiting to encourage people and to pursue it to set them free, much like He did while He was here. Follow the example and don't give up. The more like Jesus you become, the more freedom you will have.

Why? Because you are real.

That's the real dream, my brotha.

chapter 13

soldier of heaven

The reason the Son of God appeared was to destroy the
devil's work.

1 JOHN 3:8

Sometimes you gotta fight.

It took a good two hours to get to the maximum security prison in Chiapas, Mexico, where eighty men were waiting for us. The majority had
been there ten years, wrongfully incarcerated by local mob bosses who
were upset with the Christians not paying for pagan rituals. The Christians upset the balance of power in this mountain community by refusing
to pay, so the local authorities went on a killing spree and framed the
Christians. The kangaroo court process was bought and paid for by the
same Mexican mafia, and the plan landed all the resisters in jail.

And here we were, five gringos from *Los Estados Unidos* bringing supplies
and encouragement to our brothers in persecution.

Guys in black jumpsuits wearing bullet-proof vests and holding M-16s met us at the gate. They took our cameras and escorted us to the processing area to get in. We'd already gone through the legal nightmare of getting them to allow us in, but we still weren't sure we had the proper paperwork. One by one we were searched up and down, passed through a metal detector, and told to wait. All the gifts we'd brought were intricately inspected—toothbrushes, soap, toilet paper.

The Mexican mafia went on a killing spree and framed the Christians.

When had all been searched, a prison escort took us through several sliding steel doors that closed behind us with a loud *boom!* Each time, the *clank* of keys, another sliding steel cage—*boom!* Finally, we made it to the cellblock courtyard, a fifteen-by-fifty yard strip of grass between two three story concrete cellblocks. We were told that the prisoners would be assembled and brought from their individual cells. We waited for thirty minutes and then heard the *clank* of the keys again. Somebody was coming. And when we saw a sharply dressed woman escorted by a prison guard (with no prisoners in tow), we knew something was up.

Our attorney friend spoke with the woman, the warden's assistant, and after a few minutes we realized we were not going to be allowed to see all of the prisoners. We could only visit with groups of ten at a time, which left enough time to visit with about half the men. We all knew we were getting snowed and that the obstacles were not the warden, the prison schedule, or the paperwork. This was spiritual. Somewhere behind the walls was a group of brothers who desperately needed encouragement.

We began to fire back. We asked to see all of the prisoners, not just ten at a time. Then we told the warden's assistant we would like to speak with her boss. We explained how far we'd traveled to be here and that we represented the families of these prisoners. The woman took it in and then disappeared—and the spiritual warfare began in earnest.

We knew it was more than a long shot, but God can open prison doors. We prayed and prayed and prayed that God's authority would allow us to visit these brothers suffering unjustly. Ten minutes later, our vigil was interrupted by a man walking toward us in a striped polo shirt and jeans—the warden. He looked nothing like what we expected. He even smiled.

We introduced ourselves and explained our dilemma. Apparently, he was the new warden, and he didn't know how these men had landed here. He was obviously touched, and he expressed surprise at hearing that we were Christians. He then said, "I am a Christian too. Please come into the main courtyard and you can visit with the entire prison population along with your brothers."

More clanking keys, more slamming doors, and men in orange jumpsuits began to appear. We were guided to the main prison yard: a dirt soccer field, basketball courts, and a small set of steps we used as a platform. The imprisoned brothers were weeping and hugging us, elated by our presence. I felt certain we were standing on holy ground. We found the leader, assembled the men, and garnered a large crowd of curious bystanders.

We were introduced and the preaching began. The circumstances, the faces, and the sounds rising in that courtyard are so real to me, even now.

Such a surreal experience, but I felt the dream of heaven surrounding this service. Jesus himself was present.

Alan spoke first, through a translator: "My Spanish is weak but the Word of God is strong." After a few minutes he punctuated his sermonette with a reminder that nothing can "separate [you] from the love of God that is in Christ Jesus our Lord." The men hung on every word.

Hector spoke next. "Everyone here is looking at you!" he exclaimed. "They need to see Christ in you here." When it was my turn, I began with a paraphrase of Joseph's declaration after his odyssey in prison: "What man intended for evil, God intended for good." I am not sure how well they understood my Spanish, but I finished with a pledge: "Your courage has given me more courage to witness for Christ. Your light is shining bright beyond these walls. You are the champions of the faith!"

None of us had slept the night before. Fireworks had exploded all night in celebration of Our Lady of Guadalupe. My friend Hans's bank card was eaten at an ATM and never seen again. Our lawyer's daughter fell ill that day. The prison guards told us that our paperwork was wrong and our visitation permit was invalid. We were met with obstacles at every turn. But when we prayed and laid down the gauntlet, we met the warden and were given the keys to his city to bring the Word of God to the starving.

The question that haunts me is, what if? What if we hadn't fought to speak to those men? What if we hadn't suited up and believed in God for a miracle? It's possible that no prison doors would have opened that day. No preaching of the Word of God to an entire prison population. No hugs. No tears. No shouts of worship on a rundown basketball court. No warrior's walk into the heart of darkness.

What if?

That's a battle my buddies and I will talk about when we're old. How we stood firm one day and how the cavalry of heaven came to the rescue.

The Ultimate Fighter

Jesus Christ came to fight and to win. Now it's true, I'm a military brat, and my mom is a survivor of a POW camp. I was saturated in a masculine mind-set and aggressive testosterone. But none of that has anything to do with this: Jesus came to wage spiritual battle and win back His hostages from the hand of the Enemy. It's all Him. It's His war. He declared a jihad against Satan and sin. This is His battle and when it comes to blows, there is real blood—lots of it. You can't read about the paranoid campaign of infanticide Herod launched to stop Christ's birth and not realize the reality. You can't see the terror in the demons He cast out and fail to understand. You can't think of the satanic assaults on His mind, listen to the Sermon on the Mount, or watch Jesus trashing the temple and write it off as an overactive pituitary gland. No. A terrifying day is coming when our jaws will drop in awe. All will behold the Rider. And He's not bringing flowers to the party.

> I saw heaven standing open and there before me was a white horse, whose rider is called Faithful and True. With justice he judges and makes war. His eyes are like blazing fire, and on his head are many crowns. He has a name written on him that no one knows but he himself. He is dressed in a robe dipped in blood, and his name is the Word of God. The armies of heaven were following him, riding on white horses and dressed in fine linen, white and clean. Out of his mouth comes a sharp sword with which to strike down the

nations. "He will rule them with an iron scepter." He treads the
winepress of the fury of the wrath of God Almighty. On his robe
and on his thigh he has this name written: KING OF KINGS AND
LORD OF LORDS. (Revelation 19:11–16)

I would hate to be on the receiving end of this Rider's sword. Jesus
Christ is vicious in the war against Satan and evil. If there are even trace
levels of testosterone in your body, thinking about that sort of Jesus
should get your adrenaline pumping. He's the embodiment of the ultimate evil fighter—invincible and quite capable of inflicting some lasting
damage. And all this from the defender of the helpless, the one so full of
love toward people that He cried tears of blood.

But you mess with His brothers, watch out.

Being God's man means being a man who is ready to engage in combat
with the Enemy. More specifically, it means being prepared to fight the
spiritual battles. The opposite of this is a casual Christian man who fails
to "take your stand against the devil's schemes" (Ephesians 6:11), a man
who capitulates on God's dream for you.

> **dream fact**
> *Jesus is the embodiment of
> the ultimate evil fighter.*

One measure of Christlikeness
is your steady commitment to
fight the unseen spiritual
enemy. Do you proactively go
after the evil and sin in your own life and others' wherever it raises its
head? Maybe you wonder how a man can be this confident. It's found in
the warrior spirit and character of Jesus, a.k.a. Lion of the Tribe of Judah,
who lives—and lives in you! This is the Man who chose death and stood
firm against the devil's assaults. And He has called you to do the same.

This is profound. God's dream for you is to possess this same soldier heart by training in His shoes. Watch His film. Study His responses. Scrutinize the Enemy's tactics. Imitate Christ and integrate His skills.

Jesus Swiftly and Effectively Resisted Satan's Appeals to His Appetites

Remember the God-Man who entered the jungle of temptation full of the Holy Spirit? That's the first key. He was whispered an offer as He looked into the face of the tempter in the wilderness. What'd He do? He unloaded both barrels by declaring, "It is written: 'Worship the Lord your God and serve him only'" (Luke 4:8).

Are you so filled with the Holy Spirit that you could also respond with force? Do you have Scripture loaded and ready in your heart? More important, do you use your weapon when tempted? The psalmist had this in mind when he wrote on the ancient scroll, "The mouth of the righteous man utters wisdom, and his tongue speaks what is just. The law of his God is in his heart; his feet do not slip" (Psalm 37:30–31).

This is your ammo as a spiritual warrior.

Jesus Recognized the Enemy's Distractions from God's Purposes in His Life

"From that time on Jesus began to explain to his disciples that he must go to Jerusalem and suffer many things at the hands of the elders, chief priests and teachers of the law.... Peter took him aside and began to rebuke him. 'Never, Lord!' he said. 'This shall never happen to you!' Jesus turned and said to Peter, 'Get behind me, Satan! You are a stumbling block to me; you do not have in mind the things of God, but the things of men'" (Matthew 16:21–23).

Peter had it all planned out: No ugly political mix-up. No nasty military coup. No religious trouble. Jesus saw beyond Peter's ill-timed gaffe. He saw Satan's scheme to divert him away from his mission. The message was a familiar whisper: "Doesn't that plan sound a whole lot better? It makes so much more sense."

> **Is God calling you to call someone out?**

Peter didn't have horns on his head, but Jesus didn't answer Peter. He spoke to Satan. This should really make us think twice about how God's man is supposed to look at people. Do you see people as subject to spiritual forces? Do you see the potential for Satan to use people around you, even familiar faces, to divert you from what you know?

Is God calling you to call someone out? Jesus knew that the devil was the messenger behind that suggestion. And He ended it. The ability to exercise this kind of discernment and courage—not to mention the sacrifice of comfort—is God's ambition for every God's man. Jesus had this sort of courage, because He knew about the Enemy and his motives. He said, "The thief comes only to steal and kill and destroy" (John 10:10). "He was a *murderer* from the beginning, not holding to the truth, for there is no truth in him. *When he lies, he speaks his native language,* for he is a liar and the father of lies" (John 8:44).

Jesus studied Satan's true character and exposed it. He knew all of these games had one thing in common: Satan, the one who doesn't change his stripes. When you're tempted, do you think, *Satan*? Or do you think, *It's only fatigue; just a weak moment*? Maybe, but that's exactly where Jesus was in His moments of temptation too. And He didn't let Satan take advantage.

Jesus Showed His Authority over the Devil—and Provided It to His Followers

"When a strong man, fully armed, guards his own house, his possessions are safe. But *when someone stronger attacks and overpowers him,* he takes away the armor in which the man trusted and divides up the spoils" (Luke 11:21–22). There is a cosmic chain of command, but Satan's lust for the top can't match the Man at the top. When Jesus made a heavenly power play, He said the same authority was available to them: "The seventy-two returned with joy and said, 'Lord, even the demons submit to us in your name.' He replied, 'I saw Satan fall like lightning from heaven. *I have given you authority* to trample on snakes and scorpions and *to overcome all the power of the enemy;* nothing will harm you" (Luke 10:17–19).

Confidence in Christ's power is more critical than equipment. When you hold a machine gun and your enemy has a sharp stick, you can have confidence. This is the sentiment Jesus passed to His men: don't worry, you have authority over evil; God has authority over all! It's not what God's man can do for God, but what Jesus Christ has done for us.

Overwhelming strength and commanding authority produces confidence. Do you walk in that power, authority, and confidence right now as God's man? Do you know how to access it and bring it into play every day? There are eager forces working hard to thwart God's work. They may be unseen, but they desperately want control and power over us. Jesus Christ has given us the intelligence and tools to fight the forces that oppose us.

You are here at this moment in history to fight in the character of Christ.

Eo Ipso

Eo ipso is a Latin term that means "by that very act." Every follower of Christ, eo ipso, is necessarily and deliberately an enemy of Satan.

Pause for a moment and let the paint dry on that one, as they say in the South. The statement is simple, easy to understand, but the implications are perilously profound. This is what makes being God's man both noble and hazardous. Of course, it's still hazardous without God, but the very act of identification with Jesus Christ means one irrefutable thing for you—you are the enemy of hell. While we might be tempted to keep this reality neatly compartmentalized, Jesus didn't. As we learned, what mattered is what He spoke and not what we wish mattered. Just the acts:

- On the nature of the battle and who is called to fight: "From the days of John the Baptist until now, the kingdom of heaven has been force-fully advancing, and forceful men lay hold of it" (Matthew 11:12).
- On man's complicity with the devil: "Why is my language not clear to you? Because you are unable to hear what I say. You belong to your father, the devil, and you want to carry out your father's desire" (John 8:43–44).
- On the reality of spiritual warfare and the impossibility of neutrality: "This is war, and there is no neutral ground. If you're not on my side, you're the enemy; if you're not helping, you're making things worse" (Matthew 12:30, MSG).

The action of knowing and loving Him makes every Christ follower the very real opposition of Satan and his forces. Jesus eliminated the option of being double-minded. As stunning as a full-scale declaration of war among nations would be, as lamentable and grievous as the costs, this war, our war, engenders cosmic consequences that dwarf every hell of every war ever fought. There is no such thing as peaceful coexistence on this one. Instead there will be violent campaigns of spiritual warfare and forceful men prosecuting them.

Are satanic forces and human beings presently cooperating to prosecute evil against God's Son and followers? Yes. That is the unpolluted reality, my brother. Are you ready?

The Man Satan Loves

What does the man Satan loves look like?

- *He swallows Satan's biggest lie.* Satan doesn't exist. He's not active. He's been overblown by the spiritual nut-jobs who see a demon under every rock.
- *He accepts only the tangible.* He feels, sees, and experiences only material things without eyes to see the great spiritual war for his life and the lives of others.
- *He doesn't realize he has weapons.* He doesn't know how to use them, when to use them, or that they even exist. (Read Ephesians 6:10–18 for basic weapon training and applications.)
- *He allows Satan to oppress him freely.* He doesn't put up a fight through criticism, guilt, doubt, fear, and discouragement. He doesn't see Satan trying to hinder his growth and effectiveness by moving him away from spiritual disciplines.
- *He doesn't know Satan's fears.* He sees no power in the presence of God, the utterance of His word, and the sound of Jesus's name.
- *He is unaware of his authority.* He has no ability to project and utilize his spiritual identity in Christ.

This is God's worst nightmare for one of His sons. But the man Satan fears has opposite basic qualities:

- *He realizes his place.* God's man knows, above all, that spiritual warfare is engaged from a position of deep love for God and people.
- *He respects his opponent.* He is personally aware of Satan, his tactics, and his power to influence lives.
- *He reveres truth.* And he can clearly spot twisted manipulations.
- *He responds decisively.* He is constantly seeking Christlike behaviors and strategies to take away Satan's angle.
- *He relies on the Holy Spirit for spiritual insight.* He knows his every choice is subject to spiritual warfare.
- *He rests in grace.* This man knows that Jesus Christ has bankrupted Satan's power.

Satan hates a guy who's on guard and sees everyday choices as tactical maneuvers. Forgiving someone versus attacking, saying no to unhealthy appetites versus feeding them, encouraging versus tearing down. Choosing not to work late versus straining family relationships. Choosing Christlike approaches to problems versus justifying different courses. The daily stuff is where the dream is worked out—day to day, moment by moment.

As a soldier of heaven, you know Satan's tactic is to wear down your resolve little by little. You know how he tries to make people too busy for quality relationships with God and others. You know your faith is a cosmic crusade with Christ leading the charge, His eyes fixed, His blade drawn. The Rider, calling to His men, "Swords to the ready!"

chapter 14

no thanks

The world is but a great inn, where we are to stay a night or
two, and be gone; what madness is it to get our heart upon
our inn, as to forget our home!

—THOMAS WATSON

I'm tempted by stuff every day. On my way to Des Moines, I had a layover in Omaha. "I would like to be the first to welcome you to Omaha
where the local time is 12:15. For those of you continuing on to Des
Moines, you are free to move around the cabin…"

Yadda, yadda, yadda. I needed a stretch after my middle seat experience
with "Gigantor" to my left and a Nebraska Cornhusker to my right.
When these two behemoths disembarked, I gulped for air and thanked
God for the ability to breathe through my mouth, saving my ability to
smell (if you know what I'm saying). Liberated from the human sandwich, I got up from my seat. After a good stretch in the back of the plane,
I remained standing and peered down the aisle as Hoss and Gigantor
deplaned. A few minutes passed while I rested my elbows on a headrest

at the back of the aisle. Head down, clasped hands, and closed eyes, I must have looked like someone managing a hangover.

> *You would have to be a robot not to notice.*

The flight attendant began to greet passengers. "Hello. Welcome aboard. Hello." I raised my head. And that's when I saw...the Creature.

A certifiable head-turner—every man, woman, and child would've had to be legally blind to miss this "legally blonde" phenomenon. If I can lay it out for you:

- six foot and some change
- short, bleached blond hair
- long black lashes
- Broadway performance makeup
- Texas-size ruby red lips
- Ferrari chassis
- short red leather vest cut to reveal Cleveland, Ohio
- fitted white capri pants
- black spike heels

In short, the Creature was surreal. As she headed down the aisle, I took it in and forced myself to reassume my head-down position. My exact thought process was this:

- *Wow.*
- *Wonder what the attention-grabbing is all about.*
- *Boy, the Enemy never quits.*
- *Thank God for Chrissy.*

It was a visual spectacle—sort of like an exotic tropical fish among average goldfish. You would have to be a robot not to notice. I'm not a robot.

My second thought related to the "why" of this creature, as in, "Why the Las Vegas cabaret show?" It was so over-the-top, I couldn't help but wonder. After a decade working in psychological health, thousands of individual assessments, and hundreds of admissions to outpatient counseling with hurting people, I had learned one thing: the bigger the show, the deeper the hurt. It doesn't matter if it's a Gothic teen wrapped in death or a superwoman sensually dressed. As sure as the rising sun, these demonstrations are not-so-thinly-veiled requests for attention.

The looks help pad a little girl's wounded search for love. How do I know this? Because I was just like Miss Omaha before Christ's love solved the dilemma. I too used to wonder, *Am I worthy of love?* And even though I knew better in the back of the plane, part of me was still vulnerable to answering the Creature's scream for attention. I was being sucked into her plight until the voice of the Spirit intervened.

It all happened in a matter of a few seconds, but I continued to keep my head lowered at half-mast, shaking it from side to side, when all of a sudden, I felt a stinging *whap* on my shoulder.

"You guys love that sort of stuff," a voice behind me whispered. It was a flight attendant who had seen me notice the Creature. She wanted me to know she knew what I was thinking.

I quickly reached into my wallet and pulled out a picture of Chrissy. "Why look at *that* when you can look at *this*?" I smiled and tapped the picture, puffing up my chest and looking directly in her eyes.

Not expecting my response, she tried to cover the stunned look on her face, muttered something about how beautiful Chrissy was, and shuttled up the aisle to greet the Creature.

Temptation had presented itself. I could have camped there, ogled her, compared her to other women, and had a little mental Happy Meal. But unlike the old Kenny, who would have gladly scarfed the whole meal and eagerly hunted for the toy prize inside, I said, "No thanks." In fact, it was a triple no to the indulgent voices of culture, my own dark side, and the devil who seeks to soft sell the consequences and make acceptance of the temptation seem benign. The Enemy loves to mask these creature comforts like the champion fisherman he is, dangling lures at just the right time and trying to conceal my number one temptation as a deserved indulgence in a moment of weakness.

Spiritual warfare is this subtle. And toxic. If God's man is not aware and not trained to see the fangs of the Enemy, Satan (and his partner, the world) will have you.

Knowledge of the battle that rages for spiritual control of my heart and mind, knowledge of how people's outside reflects their inside, and knowledge of a better hope for my life all combined for my narrow victory on that layover. These are the tactics that allow God's man to reframe the picture of people and circumstances, to decode the spiritual realities, and to take risks in the direction of his hope—in Christ. I tell guys all the time, "It's not a sin to be tempted. It's a sin to RSVP!"

As we live in the world, we risk saying no to temptation in order to say yes to God.

Connecting Flights

Layovers are not home. It doesn't matter whether it is a mental layover with a Creature on the tarmac in Omaha or a physical layover en route to my final destination. These are not home. Chrissy is home. I don't invest or take risks where I don't live. These excursions are not the hope for me. I say "no thanks" to them because I place my emotional, relational, and physical capital into my real home.

It's about remembering who you are—and whose you are. It's the knowledge of where you come from and where you are going that's essential for practical, day-to-day Christian faith. When you have clearly settled the answers to these questions, you can be spiritually aggressive without apology—even ruthless with respect to personal commitments and boundaries.

God's man can risk mightily for his hopes and dreams—but always in the direction of home.

Think about it. You hoped you could win the affections of your bride, so you risked asking her on a first date and acted like you were in touch with your feelings (which apparently worked). Another time, you hoped you could land that job promotion, so you risked preparing yourself and calling on your inner strength to make the best case. Maybe you'd made a commitment to a physical training routine in hopes of entering a marathon or finishing an endurance challenge. Maybe it was for a start-up business or a new home that convinced you to invest. You risked relational, emotional, physical, and financial capital in hopes of starting something new. And you did it in hopes of creating an ongoing place you could call "home."

We always risk with the end in mind.

I have the awesome privilege of doing frequent chapel services for professional sports teams. I love it, especially because I get to take one of my kids. I will never forget the time Ryan and I flew to Oakland to be with the New York Jets. Right before we were about to board the plane my son said, "Dad, I don't feel so good." *No. Not now.* But my worst fears were realized—stomach flu. Did it stop him? No way. Dinner with Jet's QB Chad Pennington and his offensive line with tickets to the following game kept my son in high hopes. He was committed to complete his dream trip either a healthy man or sick as a dog. He hoped in spite of his physical discomfort.

> *You hoped you could win the affections of your bride, so you acted like you were in touch with your feelings.*

I read of a time Michael Jordan was struck with the stomach flu like Ryan. His bout with the virus came right before critical game six in the NBA championships. He didn't tell anyone but pushed through, played the entire game, and made the buzzer-beating shot to win for the Chicago Bulls.

We take big fat honking risks in the areas of our greatest hopes despite great personal costs. Pain is a powerful deterrent and has the ability to erode our confidence. But while discomfort might dissuade, in a head-to-head battle, I'll take hope in the dream every time.

Jesus came from God as a citizen of heaven. He longed for the time He would return home. His cure for worldliness was always bringing to mind His true home, the eternal place He knew was far more glorious than whatever He was giving up for it. He impressed upon others His personal knowledge of heaven and His awareness of its promise for all who would believe. And by His choices to risk earth for heaven, we got a clear picture of who He was and where He was headed, making what He might have possessed instead or what was said about Him by people pale in insignificance. Everyone who Christ encountered saw it: that firm gaze on an eternal kingdom that made it easy to say "no thanks" to every temptation away from His true home. Jesus was not worldly, because this world was not His home, not His hope.

The big question for you today is this: what are your greatest hopes in this life? The risks you take tell all. If you love people, you will take risks to make those relationships healthy and intimate. By contrast, if you love heroin, you manipulate, steal, and take inconceivable risks to get more money to get back to your home—the next fix. But if you love God, you take risks with your choices that show where you are from and where you are headed.

God's man, like the God-Man, risks forceful choices in the direction of his ultimate hope of heaven.

An Attacking Hope

God's dream for our lives is Christlikeness. Christlikeness involves hard choices in the direction of our hopes of our eternal home.

The Constitution of Christ was this: always say no to the offerings of earth if they diminish the values or relationships of our homes. Christ's clear statement was that earth is a layover. That perspective produces a very practical spiritual paradigm of spiritual aggression that views choices on earth as an investment in our homes and hopes.

The Sermon on the Mount is Article I: "Don't hoard treasure down here where it gets eaten by moths and corroded by rust or—worse!—stolen by burglars. Stockpile treasure in heaven, where it's safe from moth and rust and burglars. It's obvious, isn't it? The place where your treasure is, is the place you will most want to be, and end up being" (Matthew 6:19–21, MSG).

Questions: Where's your home? Where do you want to end up? On my flight layovers, everybody I see really wants to get home to family, friends, their own bed. Same for the God-Man. He kept choosing to say no to things on the layover. And at the same time, He was saying yes to home. During this layover, God's man says:

- *No to indulgence.* "The Devil, playing on his hunger, gave the first test: 'Since you're God's Son, command this stone to turn into a loaf of bread.' Jesus answered by quoting Deuteronomy: 'It takes more than bread to really live' " (Luke 4:3–4, MSG). The God-Man had appetites He chose not to feed for higher purposes. Especially when those appetites ran counter to God's Word home. This was a pattern for Him on earth whether it was food, sex, shelter, or other physical comforts—"But we have one who has been tempted in every way, just as we are—yet was without sin" (Hebrews 4:15). His bodily needs on earth never had more authority over His intuitions toward home and relationships there. His spiritual purposes always satisfied more deeply and could not be sold out for a piece of toast.

- *No to another job.* "For the second test he led him up and spread out all the kingdoms of the earth on display at once. Then the Devil said, 'They're yours in all their splendor to serve your pleasure. I'm in charge of them all and can turn them over to whomever I wish. Worship me and they're yours, the whole works.' Jesus refused, again backing his refusal with Deuteronomy: 'Worship the Lord your God and only the Lord your God. Serve him with absolute single-heartedness'" (Luke 4:5–8, MSG). The God-Man was not going to wear a split jersey—half for heaven, half for hell. He wanted to honor His heavenly contract, no matter what. No escape clauses, no provisos, no loopholes were sought. In fact, He flatly rejected them. Jesus reveled in being a one-team guy—even though He was living in a different town for a while. He reminded twisted agents of the rules in His contract whenever they came calling.

> **dream fact**
> *Jesus chose to save his competitive juices for where they really counted.*

- *No to wasting influence.* "For the third test the Devil took him to Jerusalem and put him on top of the Temple. He said, 'If you are God's Son, jump. It's written, isn't it, that "he has placed you in the care of angels to protect you; they will catch you; you won't so much as stub your toe on a stone"?' 'Yes,' said Jesus, 'and it's also written, "Don't you dare tempt the Lord your God"'" (Luke 4:9–12, MSG). Jesus knew a dig when He heard one and did not dignify them. Digs at His ego were a sign of weakness, not strength. Goading the God-Man seemed to make His enemies look weaker and Him better. It always backfired. Calling Jesus a wuss or daring Him may have made Him clench a fist or a jaw or think about how He was gonna take care of the Tempter at a later time, but He never honored it with a reaction. He simply wasn't going to do it. What a waste of His influence and energy it would have been on earth. That was not the legacy He wanted to leave for the folks at home. Instead, He chose to save the competitive juices for where they really counted.

- *No to pride.* "Teacher, we know you have integrity, that you are indifferent to public opinion, don't pander to your students, and teach the way of God accurately" (Mark 12:14, MSG). Earth was a business trip with some key meetings, lots of training of the core team, and a major acquisition of the competition's holdings. He had a holy indifference to criticism and flattery. He had been sent by the Boss and He didn't much care for the agendas of others if it compromised the one that mattered in the boardroom back home. He didn't cultivate a love for the airport terminal. He focused on the contacts He wanted to make and ignored the incidental trappings.

- *No to a change of itinerary.* " 'Tell us: Is it lawful to pay taxes to Caesar or not?' He knew it was a trick question and said, 'Why are you playing these games with me? Bring me a coin and let me look at it.' They handed him one. 'This engraving—who does it look like? And whose name is on it?' 'Caesar,' they said. Jesus said, 'Give to Caesar what is his, and give God what is his.' Their mouths hung open, speechless" (Mark 12:14–17, MSG). Many did not want the God-Man to make His gate for His flight home. Jesus always showed these men whose picture was on His passport, reminding them whose stamp validated where He was going.

- *No to physical concerns.* "Going a little ahead, he fell on his face, praying, 'My Father, if there is any way, get me out of this. But please, not what I want. You, what do *you* want?'… Again he prayed, 'My Father, if there is no other way than this, drinking this cup to the dregs, I'm ready. Do it your way' " (Matthew 26:39, 42, MSG). Jesus's

layover on earth was not without real moments of feeling disconnected, the biggest stranger in the world. The isolation got to Him,
infected His spirit, and caused fever and nausea—especially before
the final flight for home. He knew He was going to feel horrible but
showed up anyway. He was getting on this flight even if it meant the
greatest physical pain imaginable the entire way. He believed—He
hoped—the sacrifice would be worth it. He reasoned it out, made
His peace with the reality of pain, and chose to board anyway. Nothing would stop Him.

Imatio Cristi

Saying no represented not an act of self-limitation but an attacking hope
involving self-denial and hard choices. These choices were focused on
Jesus's final destination, not on the layover. He was just passing through.
Through personal sacrifice, Jesus arrived at the greatest prize.

This lifestyle is God's dream for us. Christ said, "Whoever follows me
will never walk in darkness" (John 8:12). In his classic work, *Imatio
Cristi (The Imitation of Christ)*, Thomas à Kempis, a fourteenth-century
monk famous for his works on following in Jesus's footsteps, broke down
the thought this way:

> By these words of Christ we are advised to imitate His life and
> habits, if we wish to be truly enlightened and free from all blindness
> of heart. Let our chief effort, therefore, be to study the life of Jesus
> Christ.... This is the greatest wisdom—to seek to the kingdom of
> heaven through contempt of the world. It is vanity, therefore, to
> seek and trust in riches that perish. It is vanity also to court honor
> and to be puffed up with pride. It is vanity to follow the lusts of the

body and to desire things for which severe punishment later must come. It is vanity to wish for long life and to care little about a well-spent life. It is vanity to be concerned with the present only and not to make provision for the things to come. It is vanity to love what passes quickly and not to look ahead to where eternal joy abides.[5]

A vanity is empty, useless, and hollow. In other words, the ineffectual life is the one investing in the layover versus the final destination. Wisdom and value for Jesus was looking ahead "to where eternal joy abides" and making decisions that reflected this ultimate horizon. The rest, in the end, was vanity, because it did not carry over to home.

To fulfill His mission on earth, Jesus had to have contempt for the opposition, and a powerful knowledge that the world was an adversary of His identity and his mission. Our bond with His mission was sealed in His own prayer for us that our full mission would come about and God's dream would be realized: "I have given them your word and the world has hated them, for they are not of the world any more than I am of the world. My prayer is not that you take them out of the world but that you protect them from the evil one. They are not of the world, even as I am not of it.... As you sent me into the world, I have sent them into the world" (John 17:14–16, 18).

> **dream fact**
> *"This is the greatest wisdom—to seek to the kingdom of heaven through contempt of the world."*

Jesus knew our layover time would follow His, but His attitude would continue on inside His men. He knew God's men would be indigenous—planted tactically in every corner of the world to fulfill God's kingdom purposes. He knew God's men would be pilgrims with a mind-set like their Brother-King, unowned by culture, empowered by His words and actions. He believed in the hope that we'd be like Him, in the world but not of it, transformed by a different spiritual DNA. We would participate in relationships but be separate, guided by higher laws. Throughout the centuries, we would assimilate, respect the governments of earth, but not align with the darkness.

Similarly, there is strong encouragement in the apostles' teachings on how to reflect Jesus's "don't take out of but be not of the world" message. Paul says, "Do not conform any longer to the pattern of this world" (Romans 12:2) yet also to "become all things to all men" (1 Corinthians 9:22). It is one of the most difficult balances in the Christian life, but as we strive for it, we become like Jesus, aliens and exiles, yet connected and indigenous for God's purposes.

God's dream for us is that we would move freely and confidently in this tension.

> And they admitted that they were aliens and strangers on earth. People who say such things show that they are looking for a country of their own. If they had been thinking of the country they had left, they would have had opportunity to return. Instead, they were longing for a better country—a heavenly one. Therefore, God is not ashamed to be called their God, for he has prepared a city for them. (Hebrews 11:13–16)

Imatio Cristi! Imatio Cristi.

chapter 15

the time has come

The riders in a race do not stop short when they reach the goal. There is a little finishing canter before coming to a standstill. There is time to hear the kind voice of friends and to say to oneself, "The work is done."

—OLIVER WENDELL HOLMES JR.

My dad didn't start strong, but he finished strong.

Bud Luck was a scrawny kid growing up in North Carolina in the twenties and thirties. He had pneumonia twice and had to relearn how to walk because he was in bed for such long periods of time. In the Depression, good medicine was hard to come by. When he would get up enough strength, he would return to school, but that was almost as hazardous as the pneumonia. Small, frail, and socially awkward, he got picked on a lot. Decades later, he told me that at recess and lunch he would hide to avoid the bullies and then sprint back to class at the second bell. We had never talked like this before, so all of it was news to me. But these revelations helped me understand the man, his relationships, his battles, and his journey with God. This was one of the first real conversations I ever had with my dad. I was thirty-nine and he was eighty-one, in the hospital for a bypass surgery. We had both waited a long time for this. He lived almost a year after that surgery, but he was never the same. His time was coming.

I got the call about a month before my dad died. I flew several times to visit him in the skilled nursing facility where he was hospitalized. He chronicled his entire life's journey for me. More and more revelations. Better and better conversations. High school sweethearts. Joining the navy after Pearl Harbor. Submarine service in Scotland. Being accepted into the V-12 business program at Harvard, then the University of Virginia, and finally the University of Pennsylvania. Chief supply positions aboard the *General Mann* and land-based assignments in Norfolk, Bayonne, and Port Magu naval bases. These were the years I didn't know much about, and they fascinated me the most. These were his glory years from a career perspective—his best days of his best years. While he reveled in his military family and ascent to the rank of lieutenant commander, his relationships with my mother, sisters, brothers, and me were full of regret. The best of times paralleled the

His time was coming.

worst. The many deployments, being unable to emotionally connect with the family when he was home, and the turbulent sixties with three teenagers who hated being in a military family all led to this sense of loss.

The final requiem to the glory days of stripes, officers' club functions, and the only order my dad ever knew in his life was his retirement in 1967 after twenty-six years of service. He was like a lot of professionals who, in hanging onto their careers so tightly, forgot how to live. Going from full-time military life to full-time family life was chaotic and terrifying to this man who was used to order and whose dad had left him to carry the mantle alone after dying from alcohol poisoning. If you are a military kid like me, you might know what I am talking about. It's like a professional football player who gets injured after a few solid years. He thought he'd be playing longer, but now he's forced to leave the only purpose he's ever known. That's one of the hardest transitions imaginable. Many get depressed and disintegrate.

Which is exactly what happened to my dad. He got a job in the private sector as a logistics engineer with a defense contractor, working with the Trident and Poseidon nuclear submarine programs. We never knew where he was going or when he would be back. He tried to make our family work, but having to face a wife and seven children was too overwhelming. That lost feeling was horrible for him after having so much order and a place to go when things at home were not good. His lack of marital and parenting skills amplified these feelings. The navy taught him how to be a good seaman and officer, but the rules that governed that career didn't work in a large family. He tried to run our house like a ship.

For my family, the seventies were a stupor of work, alcohol, and malaise. No one was connecting, interacting, hugging, or communicating. We each found our alternatives as my dad withdrew into a private routine, waking up at 4:30, drinking before work, working until 4:00, eating dinner, watching the news, and going to bed. His life was like the movie *Groundhog Day,* reliving the same day over and over. Yet instead of progressing, he was growing more bitter and depressed and medicating with alcohol. In 1984, the family decided it was time for an intervention. Dad went to a rehab program and was discharged only to relapse again in three months. He was readmitted and his boss gave him an ultimatum. This time it stuck, and his Alcoholics Anonymous meetings took over the routine.

For the first time in my dad's life, he had found a community of people who talked about what they were going through. For an emotionally challenged navy guy, this was nothing short of a miracle. The best part of this second tour of rehab was that my dad began to explore spiritual disciplines connected to his recovery and laid the foundation for an interesting discussion one Christmas break during my sophomore year at UCLA. I

> *His life was like the movie* **Groundhog Day,** *reliving the same day over and over.*

just happened to have a gospel tract called the *Four Spiritual Laws* in my pocket as I broached the subject of his recovery. I was twenty years old and he was sixty-five. The conversation progressed from discussing a higher power who could "restore us to sanity" to a Bible passage that read, "For there is one God and one mediator between God and men, the man Christ Jesus, who gave himself as a ransom for all men" (1 Timothy 2:5–6). The higher power had a name, and it was Jesus Christ. My dad prayed with me that night to invite Christ into his life as his higher power. Dad began the fourth quarter of life with a touchdown reception from a perfectly placed pass by our MVP.

What happened next? Morphing happened. Subtle and profound transformations, visible changes from the withdrawn bald guy we had come to know and loathe. A new man at sixty-five, finally learning how to connect with people. The new routine of a man who knew his time was short. Over the next sixteen years, my dad fought to the finish:

- pulling my kids onto his lap, no longer annoyed or bothered by them
- volunteering to pray at family gatherings, leaving everyone in tears
- preparing himself for when we'd have to go home, always asking when we first arrived, "When do you have to leave?"

- writing personal notes to the family asking for forgiveness for the lost years
- patience and fewer arguments with Mom—even surprising tenderness at the end
- "I love you" regularly spoken
- lots more smiles

My dad had become a real man and a great guy to be around. Everyone loved going places with him. He was a party machine. He would ask my siblings, "Where ya going? Can I come?" like a kid just excited to be with us. Morphing was happening.

We buried my father with full military honors. Veterans of his Seabees Unit were present, along with the navy funeral detail, and it was a solemn honor. They rang the ship bell and took roll call. With each peal of the sonorous bell, each sailor's name and rank was called and each sailor responded. Then the bell and the name Lieutenant Commander William E. Luck. Silence. The bell rang again and again his name was called. On the third ring, the navy chaplain stepped forward.

"Lieutenant Commander William E. Luck is not present, sir. He has been reassigned to the office of the Supreme Commander."

The last sixteen years of my dad's life made it a unique moment. He finished strong, and when the final bell tolled signaling his departure to the Supreme Commander, no one thought about the lost years. He had what we never thought possible—life with God. His dream had come true.

And I saluted him.

"Father, the Time Has Come"

Jesus Christ was the consummate finisher. He held back certain aspects of His divine agenda, practicing self-discipline, guarding the information for just the right time to share. He restrained His power until the end drew nearer, and then He began to reveal more about His plan. In the gospel of John, leading up to Christ's crucifixion, we read five times that something had not happened because His time "had not yet come" (see John 2:4; 7:6, 8, 30; 8:20). An efficient steward, Jesus was building up to a final flourish that no one has ever matched. He stewarded all aspects of His life to God's ultimate plan, and at the end, He looked into His Dad's face and finally said, "Father, the time has come."

> **dream fact**
> *God's man is driven by an exceptional destiny.*

The picture we get of Jesus is movement toward His ultimate destiny. Every man wants to finish strong, but few do—Christian leaders included. Yet God's dream is for our lives to be driven by an exceptional destiny, mirroring that of Christ's as a born finisher.

At the end of His life, Jesus was like a soldier embarking on a final epic battle. He reflected on what He had accomplished, and He was eager to finish strong. Read here as John's gospel describes His final hours.

Jesus Walked Meaningfully with God to the End

"Father, the time has come. Glorify your Son, that your Son may glorify you" (John 17:1). Everything He'd previously done coalesced in this final act. He did it all for His Father: every sacrifice, every prayer, every healing, every message, every interaction. His life made perfect sense in the context of this—it was the wrap-up of a life lived well for God. This is how we can all finish when we partner meaningfully with the Holy Spirit. Above all, we can glorify God by how we finish.

Jesus Used His Specific Influence for God's Purposes

"For you granted [Jesus] authority over all people that he might give eternal life to all those you have given him. Now this is eternal life: that they may know you, the only true God, and Jesus Christ, whom you have sent" (John 17:2–3). Jesus was given authority to influence people for eternity in a specific historical, geographical, and ethnic context. To faithfully steward that God-given authority, He used His influence to consistently honor God with His life of service. Your life, too, is not one of compartmentalized contributions. It is a complete lifestyle. Finishing well requires a unified focus—a steady and disciplined consistency of commitment to allow God to use you wherever you are.

Jesus Was "On Mission"

"I have brought you glory on earth by completing the work you gave me to do" (John 17:4). When you're "on mission," you are not at home. Earth is an extended camping trip—a place you're visiting for a while to engage and then to leave. No one buys a bunch of stuff and settles in on a camping trip. No, you make do and focus on what you are there for— exploring, discovering, creating, adventure. Jesus was similarly focused, doing those things He could before He left. On earth He could bring God glory through His actions. In heaven, His chance to work for the Father on earth would be over. Jesus was not concerned with comfort, power, wealth, or enjoyment.

You finish well by striving to bring Him glory in all you are, have, and do and by completing His assignment with your particular skills, passions, personality, and experiences.

Jesus Looked Forward to His Father's Smile

"And now, Father, glorify me in your presence with the glory I had with you before the world began" (John 17:5). Completing a job well distinguishes a man and leaves a lasting impression. Jesus impressed His Dad. He defeated sin and secured salvation for all men. His relationship with the Father would take on that old familiar rhythm, free of earth's gravity. Jesus had nothing to prove to anybody, allowing Him to finish strong in the days and moments following these words. He didn't have to make His case to His critics or explain the kingdom. Now it was time for the transaction at the cross, crushing death's power, and returning home. He would leave it all on the field and enjoy the afterglow.

Jesus Trained Others to Carry God's Purposes Forward

"I have revealed you to those whom you gave me out of the world. They were yours; you gave them to me and they have obeyed your word. Now they know that everything you have given me comes from you. For I gave them the words you gave me and they accepted them. They knew with certainty that I came from you, and they believed that you sent me.... My prayer is not for them alone. I pray also for those who will believe in me through their message" (John 17:6–8, 20). A Father deploys His Son. His Son comes to earth and trains more sons. And to this day, the spiritual chain reaction has not died. Our purpose is to reach and train other men to live for God and fulfill His purposes. Jesus's method was with men: selecting them, consecrating them, and imparting His insights to them. He demonstrated, delegated, and supervised. And He reproduced His kingdom through them. It was a reciprocal interaction.

Finishing Well

Finishing well and fulfilling God's ultimate dream for your life means disciplining yourself like Jesus did during your camping trip on earth. Jim

Rohn comments on the value of discipline and finishing well when he says, "Discipline weighs ounces while regret weighs tons." Think about it. Discipline in your commitment to being God's man and living out God's dream of Christlikeness will far outweigh the regret of getting to the end and wishing you had. The apostle Paul started wrong but finished right, saying at the end, "I have fought the good fight, I have finished the race, I have kept the faith"

> *Discipline in your commitment to being God's man and living out God's dream of Christlikeness will far outweigh the regret of getting to the end and wishing you had.*

(2 Timothy 4:7). King Saul in the Old Testament started right and finished wrong saying at the end, "Surely I have acted like a fool and have erred greatly" (1 Samuel 26:21). And the Sons of Korah in Psalms declare, "This God is our God for ever and ever; he will be our guide even to the end" (Psalm 48:14).

Barriers and Boosts

If staying disciplined is critical to fulfilling God's ultimate dream for us, we should look at the barriers and study how great leaders have overcome them to finish well. A finisher is rare. Even in the Bible, you can write off roughly two-thirds of all leaders from how they ended up. Only one-third were able to avoid the pitfalls that have derailed men for centuries. In my interactions with leaders, there are common denominators that cause them to fall before reaching the finish line:

- moral failure caused by a lack of authenticity and accountability
- financial concerns that prevented acceptance of their mission
- positional or power struggles over a title within a hierarchy

- spiritual atrophy when basic devotional disciplines diminish
- intellectual stagnation—they simply stopped learning

These patches of quicksand are avoidable if love for Christ and pursuit of God's dream remain the most important focus. Each is rooted in pride, making men unwilling to submit fully to God's plan, whether it's in worship, fellowship accountability, spiritual discipline, or learning to change.

Those who finish well have:

- *a personal mission.* He learns about God's priorities in the world and eagerly aligns his skills and talents with them to the end.
- *consistent spiritual discipline.* He has a steady (not flashy) commitment to prayer, study, worship, community, accountability, service, and sharing the good news.
- *a teachable spirit.* He takes notes, listens, and integrates new truth daily from multiple sources.
- *an urgency trained on eternity.* He managers his time well, taught by God to number his days.
- *an active search for more of heaven, less of earth.* He's past proving anything to anyone. He has an audience of One. He has stopped caring what people think.

He Died Climbing

There's an epitaph for a Swiss mountain guide that stands at the bottom of the mountain that claimed his life. It reads, "He died climbing."

This should be our goal as God's men each day as we move away from our base camp on earth toward home—that we died climbing toward

God's call to become like Christ. Paul had this mind-set when he penned this ascent from a prison cell: "Not that I have already obtained all this, or have already been made perfect, but I press on to take hold of that for which Christ Jesus took hold of me. Brothers, I do not consider myself yet to have taken hold of it. But one thing I do: Forgetting what is behind and straining toward what is ahead, I press on toward the goal to win the prize for which God has *called me heavenward in* Christ Jesus" (Philippians 3:12–14).

Paul's goal was Christ. He's in a holy death grip. Bound by Christ, Paul grips Jesus's arm, and together they climb higher. Are you in Jesus's grip today?

Paul's past is settled. He can't lose regret, but he can, through Christ, eliminate its power over his pursuit. Have you settled your past? Paul is dying to himself as he climbs, keeping his eyes on the prize. So the question is: Are you gaining more of heaven by losing earth? Has your heart tipped toward heaven so much that heaven is all you see? "All of us who are mature should take such a view of things" (Philippians 3:15). Don't be complacent; there are new heights to be scaled.

> *"Forgetting what is behind and straining toward what is ahead, I press on..."*

God's dream is to see you reach that summit.

notes

1. Walt Henrichsen, *Thoughts from the Diaries of a Desperate Man: A Daily Devotional* (El Cajon, CA: Leadership Foundation, 1999), 229.
2. This story is condensed from wikipedia.org/wiki/John_McCain.
3. Paul Carano, *The Complete History of Guam* (Rutland, VT: Charles E. Tuttle, 1964), 271–72.
4. John Forbes, "I Hope My Journey with AIDS Touches Your Heart," *Purpose Driven* (2006), www.purposedriven.com/en-US/HIVAIDS Community/RecommendedReading/I_hope_my_journey_with_AI DS_touches_your+heart.htm. Used by permission of the author.
5. Thomas à Kempis, *The Imitation of Christ* (Nashville: Thomas Nelson, 1999), 1–2.